M000207051

BRINGING HOME
THE
BRIDE

BRINGING HOME
THE
BRIDE

DANIEL G. BERNARD

Whitaker House

Unless otherwise indicated, all Scripture quotations are taken from the *King James Version* (KJV) of the Bible.

Scripture quotations marked (NIV) are from the Holy Bible, *New International Version*, © 1973, 1978, 1984, International Bible Society. Used by permission.

Scripture quotations marked (AMP) are from the *Amplified New Testament*, ©1954, 1958, 1987, by the Lockman Foundation, and are used by permission; or are from the *Amplified Bible, Old Testament*, © 1962, 1964 by Zondervan Publishing House, and used by permission.

BRINGING HOME THE BRIDE

Copyright © 1995 by:
    Daniel Bernard
    Full House Ministries
    Rt. 2 Box 2040
    New Waverly, TX 77358

ISBN: 0-88368-371-7
Printed in the United States of America

Whitaker House
580 Pittsburgh Street
Springdale, PA 15144

No part of this book may be reproduced or transmitted in any form or by any means, electronic or mechanical, including photocopying, recording, or by any information storage and retrieval system, without permission in writing from the publisher.

1 2 3 4 5 6 7 8 9 10 11 / 05 04 03 02 01 00 99 98 97 96 95

TABLE OF CONTENTS

DEDICATION

To my bride Kathy, who by example has taught me unconditional love.

I would also like to thank: Grace Chapel for allowing me to preach the first part of this book, Peggy Denson for her typing, David and Lisa Panak for their editing, Pastor Ronnie Guynes for his counsel, Whitaker House for taking the chance on an unknown, and of course the Holy Spirit for the revelation of this book.

Preface

Are you someone who

...after being newly converted, had a spontaneous and bold witness that has now waned, and you need encouragement to recover your first love?

...while in an evangelism program, was zealous, but since its conclusion, your witness has fizzled?

...attends a congregation that started evangelism campaigns now non-existent?

...needs to know what God wants and has wanted since the beginning of time?

Reading this book will answer these questions and others, rekindling your desire to be a testimony of God's love. What this book will give you, above all else, is God's perspective. God's perspective is what you need to keep the evangelism fires burning within you.

There are many books on evangelism that give good insight and practical guidelines. However, knowing the "how-to" without a heart for God is like someone giving you a driver's manual for a car that has no engine.

7

Though I give practical instruction in this book, above all, my hope is that the heart of God—and what should be the heart of the church—would be imparted to you.

There are several ways in which we can read and apply God's Word: subjectively, contextually, literally, and figuratively. I will figuratively examine Genesis 24; the story of Abraham's servant, Eliezer, getting a bride for Isaac. Many events in the Old Testament are shadows of the reality found in the New Testament, and they also speak figuratively to us today.

I believe that Genesis 24 is a parallel of God's desire to have His bride. Abraham symbolically represents God the Father through being served and respected. Isaac represents the Son of God, Jesus Christ. He is the one who is waiting for his bride and for prophesy to be fulfilled. The servant is symbolic of the work of the Holy Spirit who, through His church, is to bring home the bride of Christ.

I focus on the servant's relationship, character, and consequent actions as he fulfills his assignment of retrieving a mate for the master's son. Through this, you will gain insight and instruction as an individual and as a member of the corporate body of Christ.

You will discover what you and the church are to be and to do to accomplish the mission of bringing home the bride of Christ. By the grace of the Holy Spirit, you will receive the passion and the power to bring home his end-time bride.

I recommend that you familiarize yourself with Abraham, Isaac, and Eliezer by reading Genesis 24 and its parallel in Isaiah 62. We pray God's blessings upon you as you read.

1

The Ultimate Purpose of Creation

Where there is no vision, the people perish.
—Proverbs 29:18

Volunteers from a nearby fishing village braved storm after storm to rescue many from drowning, and those who were saved often joined the rescue corps.

The volunteers offered advice to improve the services. One suggestion was to have summer practice. After training, they were able to save even more lives. However, having to drag their boats from the village for each emergency, the volunteers wasted time. So, one of the volunteers suggested building a boathouse near the coast. After a time, a third volunteer suggested that they build a shelter for the people they rescued because they often died from the cold. Another volunteer recommended adding a kitchen. With a kitchen, they could make soup to warm the storm victims. All of these innovations added to the effectiveness of their work.

So that the volunteers would be immediately available for emergencies, a rescuer suggested that they wait in the boathouse during the storms. To alleviate boredom while waiting, another volunteer recommended adding a game room. The rescue station grew in prestige, and many more joined it for that reason.

As time passed, one member observed that rescuing was a highly specialized task. He believed that only those highly trained for it should be allowed to do the job. So, they hired young men to go out in the storm while the rest cheered them on from the rescue complex.

Finally, the members had a meeting and decided to discontinue the lifesaving of the "club" altogether. It was too costly, and they were all too busy with related committee meetings and other activities.

A number protested that they had abandoned their primary purpose, so they resigned and started a real lifesaving station down the coast. Once again, they went out into the storm and waves to rescue those who were drowning.[1]

*****

Tragically, the story continued to repeat.

This parable paints an accurate picture of the church throughout history. Believers who are on fire for Christ and saving those drowning in a sea of sin somehow get side tracked into extracurricular activity which has nothing to do with rescuing the lost.

As believers, we should be saying, "I do not want to waste anything. Let my life, all that I am, and all that I have, count." For this to happen, we need to ask God for His perspective and for His vision.

A driver listens to the radio and hears the announcer say, "Let's go to our sky cab for a traffic report." A reporter circling the city in a helicopter relays to the listening audience where the traffic jams are and how to avoid them. The helicopter gives a vantage point that the driver would not normally have. With this perspective, the driver can avoid being delayed or immobilized by the heavy traffic. With God's perspective, we can also keep from being immobilized in our witness.

The church often gets caught up in programs and activities that have nothing to do with our vision. We get busy with our own lives, and we forget our purpose. We often lose sight of why God has placed us in a particular job, in a particular neighborhood, or even on the face of the earth.

The Bible says, "Where there is no vision, the people perish" (Prov. 29:18). The word *perish* literally means to "waste away." Without a vision, God's people waste their time, energy, and talent. A church without a vision will also see the lost perishing rather than being redeemed.

The Bible is a record of what God wants for His creation, and one thing that stands out from Genesis to Revelation is that God wants continued fellowship with His people. It was not good for man to be alone. Why? Man, who was created in God's image, had a need and a desire for fellowship. God is self-sufficient. He, as the Father, Son, and Holy Spirit, has sufficient fellowship. Therefore, He does not need our fellowship, but He *wants* our fellowship. God expresses His desire to have communion and fellowship with His creation by using the analogy of a bridegroom and bride—the most intimate relationship on the earth.

Throughout the Old Testament, Scripture speaks of Israel being the bride of God. Israel was called to be a holy bride that would let the nations know of the one true God. When Jesus, the bridegroom, came, He was coming for His bride. The Messiah was on the earth to call His people together.

Instead of being joined with Him, we find that the Jews did not accept Jesus. Isaiah

14

prophesied, "He is despised and rejected of men." (Isa. 53:3). John 1:11 reports, "He came unto His own, and His own received Him not." He came for His bride, but he could not unite with her because the people of Israel had prostituted themselves. Being a jealous husband, He wanted a people solely for himself. Jesus tells us, through the parables, that the kingdom has been opened to the Gentiles. Jesus brings forth the bride through his own death on the cross. He pays the debt for the sin of mankind so that His bride can come to Him.

According to 1 Peter 2:10, those who were no people had become a people. We have become the people of God. We have become the bride of Christ. We have a wedding day coming when the marriage will be consummated.

From Genesis to Revelation, we find that what God wants is to have a bride, a people that will love Him as He loves them. He entered the stream of human history for this one purpose: to claim His beloved. No one sums it up better than the late Paul Billheimer in his book, *Destined for the Throne:*

> The final and ultimate outcome and goal of events from eternity to eternity, the finished product of all the ages, is the spotless Bride of Christ united with Him in wedded bliss at the Marriage Supper of the Lamb....[2]

15

Therefore, those who make up that bride have the very heart of the bridegroom. Those who have His heart know what He wants. They have His perspective and act upon it by going out to claim more people to make up His bride. This is our calling as a church. This is why we exist. This is why we are the bride of Christ.

2

A Servant's Perspective

*But thou shalt go unto my country, and to my
kindred, and take a wife unto my son Isaac.*
—Genesis 24:4

We find in Genesis a story of a servant
who has been sent to get a bride for
his master's son. To parallel this
story to present times and our mission for
Christ's bride, Abraham, the master, represents God the Father. Isaac, the son, represents the Son of God, Jesus Christ, and
Eliezer, the servant, represents the work of
the Holy Spirit through the body of Christ to
bring home His bride.

Because of the long-term relationship
that the servant had with Abraham and Isaac,
he gained a perspective of the awesome importance and responsibility of obtaining a bride

for Isaac. Through our relationship with God, we will gain the heart to win a bride for Christ.

During Eliezer's many years with Abraham, he had witnessed Abraham's sufferings, and he saw Abraham leave everything to fulfill the promise that God had given him. The promise was that Abraham would become the father of many nations (Gen. 12). When the fulfillment of the promise was delayed, Abraham began to take the matter into his own hands. He thought the promise would be fulfilled through Eliezer.

In a petition to the Lord, Abraham says of Eliezer, "One born in my house is mine heir" (Gen. 15:3). Abraham attempted to adopt him as his son, but the word of the Lord came saying, "This shall not be thine heir; but he that shall come forth out of thine own bowels shall be thine heir" (Gen. 15:4). Still, Eliezer was like a son to Abraham.

Also, Sarah was beyond her childbearing years, yet the child was to come from Abraham's seed. Therefore, Sarah assumed that her younger maidservant, Hagar, must bear the child, and she tells Abraham to marry her. Through Hagar, Abraham has a son called Ishmael, but Ishmael was not to be the son of promise. Finally, ninety-nine-year-old Abraham had given up all hope that the promise would be fulfilled, but three angels appeared.

The angels spoke to Abraham saying that within a year he would have a child. As the angels foretold, a year from then, they had a child whom they named Isaac. As the child grew, the promise seemed secure until tested by the very words of the promise giver, "Take now thy son, thine only son Isaac, whom thou lovest...and offer him there for a burnt offering" (Gen. 22:2).

Eliezer saw Abraham struggle with the prospect of sacrificing Isaac. Abraham raised the knife to plunge it into the heart of his one and only son. However, an angel stopped him, and God provided a ram for the sacrifice.

God the Father watched as His son suffered. Through God's Word, we see Christ sweating blood as he prays during His battle in the garden of Gethsemane. We read of the ridicule that He suffered as He was spit upon and beaten beyond recognition. We know that he suffered, died, arose, and ascended into heaven. God the Father sent His only begotten son, Jesus Christ, so that through Christ's blood His bride would become spotless and could be brought home.

Through witnessing his master's sufferings, Eliezer knew the need to bring home a bride. He saw that Abraham was old and stricken in age, and Sarah, his wife, was dead. There was no chance of another child, but the promise Abraham had lived for had yet to be fulfilled. Eliezer knew that everything hinged on Isaac getting a bride and that it was up to him, the servant, to do it. What a responsibility! What a privilege!

Today's servant church is in the last days of the earth's existence. Time is running out. The bridegroom is about to descend from heaven to take back His bride. Yet, we find that at least 2.5 billion people are without a living witness of Jesus Christ among them, and many more are without a saving relationship with Jesus Christ. We must bring home the bride.

After knowing how God the Father and Son have been grieved by mankind in the past, not being involved in the desire of their hearts can only be viewed as callous, careless, and sinful. Like Abraham, God has no other way planned to get a bride. He plans to use you, His servant, to meet the present need. It is our awesome privilege and responsibility. You and I have the honor of bringing home the bride for our Lord Jesus Christ. The laborers are few, but there is nothing more important.

In his book *True Discipleship*, William MacDonald shows how some great men viewed this responsibility and privilege. President Coolidge asked John Mott, a well-known missionary/statesman, to serve as ambassador to Japan. Mott replied, "Mr. President, since God called me to (be) an ambassador of His, my ears have been deaf to all other calls."[1]

Throughout church history, God has worked with His people to bring home the bride. God raised up Luther to bring forth the reformation. Calvin, Swingli, John Knox, John Huss, Zinzendorff, Wesley, Finney, and Moody were used to purify the church and redirect it towards the goal of bringing forth His bride. As we enter the last days, God continues to use His people to bring home the bride, and he grieves the churches' divisions, doctrinal wars, heresies, and heretics.

However, God delights in you and is personally involved and concerned with your welfare: "As the bridegroom rejoiceth over the bride, so shall thy God rejoice over thee" (Isa. 62:5).

To get the full understanding of Isaiah 62:5, let's examine the New Testament parallel spoken by Jesus in Luke 15:10, "Likewise, I say unto you, there is joy in the presence of the angels of God over one sinner that repenteth." Note who is doing the rejoicing. It is not the angels (although I am sure they are rejoicing), but there is rejoicing in the midst of angels. Who is in the middle of the angels? Jesus! My God, Jesus, King of Kings, Creator rejoices over you and each sinner who repents. Is it not exciting that a member of the body can cause God to stand up and shout by bringing one to Christ!

Luke 5:10 says, "From henceforth thou shalt catch men." The word *catch* means "to snare" or "to take alive like one catching fish in a net."[2] This word is found only one other time in the New Testament: in 2 Timothy 2:26, Paul tells Timothy to instruct gently people who have fallen so that they may escape the *snare* of the devil. Satan wants *to snare* men, but God wants *to take men alive.* Therefore, we must *catch* men for Christ. Those taken by Christ are not only precious souls but potential soul winners.

God views those who arise and shine and take salvation to the nations as a crown of glory in the hand of the Lord and a royal diadem in the hand of God (Isa. 62:3). In other words, you are precious to the Lord. God cares very much about you. He is personally going to keep you. The nations will see your righteousness and kings your glory.

The servant, Eliezer was successful. He brought home a bride for the father and son. Imagine a rickety, toothless Abraham saying, "Well done, faithful servant." One can only imagine the rejoicing as the promise was fulfilled.

One day, we will actually have such an experience on a much higher level. We will see the joy on the face of our bridegroom who has waited for the arrival of His bride. He will rejoice over you, not only as part of His bride but also as one who brought home the bride.

Now, that is perspective.

3

The Relationship of Master to Servant

*And the servant put his hand under the thigh
of Abraham his master, and swore to him
concerning that matter.*
—*Genesis 24:9*

My wife, Kathy, and I have been married since 1983. We attended seminary together, pastored two churches, evangelized in a street ministry, and have been missionaries to Nigeria, W. Africa since 1991. Also, by God's grace, we have had five children; Leah, Luke, Bethany, Faith, and Peter.

We have had our highs and lows, failures and victories. We have prayed, cried, and laughed together. These experiences have brought us into a deep relationship. If you were to ask me about Kathy, I would be able to tell you about her because I know her by experience, not because I went to seminary or read a book that gives general information on wives. I live and communicate with her on a daily basis. I know her ins and outs, her plans, her hopes, her fears. I know everything about my wife, and I can tell you instantly what you need to know.

This is how we tell others about Jesus Christ. This is evangelism. I cannot tell you about God unless I know God. I cannot get others to put their trust in Him if I have not learned to trust Him. I must know God to make Him known. I cannot give to someone else what I do not have. Becoming a Christian is getting to know the person of Christ, not a creed or set of religious dogmas.

It is impossible to evangelize without a relationship with God. The very core of evangelism is revealing God to a lost and dying world. To glorify God is to reveal Him as He is.

When we think of evangelism, we picture some joyful, wide-eyed, zealous new convert. They have a testimony and a relationship with Jesus, but they do not know God to the degree of someone who has walked years by the Spirit. The new Christian cannot reveal the very character and personhood of God in the same way as someone who is older in the faith. Daniel 11:32 states that the people who know their God shall be strong and do exploits. Who really knows God? Is it the new convert or the individual who has walked with God for ten or twenty years?

In Genesis 24:2, we find a description of Abraham's servant. He was the eldest servant of the house, and he ruled over all that Abraham had. This indicates that he was probably the most mature, faithful, and loyal servant. These qualities developed through time spent with Abraham. The mature believer has demonstrated loyalty, faithfulness, and commitment, and this believer is the most qualified to do evangelism just as Eliezer was the most qualified to search for Isaac's bride.

Who can demonstrate God better than the one who has spent years learning of God and taking on His character and ministry? Unfortunately, we often find the opposite in the church. Rather than the older people leading the way in evangelism, they often are a source of discouragement not only to the young convert but to anyone who desires to evangelize.

I remember being a zealous new convert. I was obnoxious for God, and I told everyone (whether they wanted to hear or not) about Jesus. The pillars of the church said, "Yes, we remember when we were like that. You take it easy. This zeal will wear off after a while, and you will become like one of us." Though I could have used more wisdom on my approach, I was genuinely excited about my new-found relationship with Jesus Christ.

In reality, lost zeal is the reflection of a lost relationship. In Keith Green's article entitled, "Zeal: The Good, the Bad, and the Ugly," he said that true zeal is "directing all our energies and enthusiasm into our relationship with the Lord and then into our relationship with our neighbor."[1] As Jesus said, the greatest commandment is to love the Lord with all your heart, mind, soul, and strength, and to love your neighbor as yourself. True zeal for God is to enthusiastically know Him. Then from the overflow of that relationship, we should desire God's vision: to see the salvation of mankind. We must have a relationship with God to do the evangelistic work of revealing Him to the world.

The four aspects of the relationship the servant, Eliezer, had with Abraham were: master to servant, owner to steward, covenant partner/friend to friend, and father to son. I believe that these aspects cover our relationship with God. You have to understand that God has a greater relationship with us than we do with Him. He is infinite, and we are finite. What does this mean? It means He can be more to us than we can be to Him. As we look at these four aspects, we need to remember that our relationship to God is as Abraham's servant's was to him.

Let us look more closely at the relationship of master to servant. Romans 6:18 says, "Being then made free from sin, ye became the servants of righteousness." We are born again, born in the Spirit, born free from sin through the blood of Jesus to become servants of righteousness. As servants of righteousness, we have no rights.

Therefore, our obedience is not optional, and evangelism is also not optional. The Great Commission is not optional either. We obey Jesus, our master, just like the servant obeyed Abraham. Going to get a bride was the servant's duty. The servant could not say, "No, Abraham. I just do not feel led today." Bringing home a bride for the Lord Jesus Christ is our duty.

Eliezer had been a servant for many years. I believe he became a free-will bond servant who, after seven years of service, had the option to go free. A free-will bond servant would choose to stay and serve his master because of his master's goodness. The Scriptures say,

> And if the servant shall plainly say, I love my master, my wife, and my children; I will not go out free: Then his master shall bring him unto the judges;

he shall also bring him to the door, or
unto the door post; and his master
shall bore his ear through with an awl;
and he shall serve him for ever.

(Ex. 21:5–6)

The boring of the servant's ear was a symbol
of the servant's love and loyalty. Thus, the
servant was marked as the master's property,
and he served the master always.

We become bond servants or free-will servants when we choose to serve God. We are
marked with a spiritual awl. We are not our
own, but we were bought with a price. The
price was the precious blood of Jesus. We no
longer belong to ourselves, but we belong to
Jesus Christ, our Lord and Master. It is our
duty as servants to obey what the Lord, our
master, has commanded. His command is, "Go
ye therefore, and teach all nations, baptizing
them in the name of the Father, and of the
Son, and of the Holy Ghost"(Matt. 28:19).

Note that this master/servant relationship is one of intimacy. You make your commitment to your master freely. You do not do
his commands merely out of duty.

In the fifteenth chapter of John, Jesus is
having one of his last intimate conversations
with his disciples before going to the cross. He
says to them,

> Henceforth I call you not servants; for
> the servant knoweth not what his lord
> doeth: but I have called you friends; for
> all things that I have heard of my Fa-
> ther I have made known unto you.
>
> (John 15:15)

Why? They had grown into an intimate friendship with Jesus through which he was able to
share and entrust details of the kingdom. Jesus
said in John 14:15, "If ye love me, keep my
commandments." As servants, we have a sense
of duty to obey, but as bond servants, we have
intimacy, and our obedience is motivated by
love for our master. We have a good master
who has set us free. He set us free from the slav-
ery and sin of Satan by His precious blood. Thus,
we, as servants with love in our hearts, gladly
fulfill the duty of bringing home the bride.

After Abraham's servant swore that he
would not take a wife for Isaac from the daughters of the Canaanites, he immediately set out
to fulfill his promise. He asked specifically for
the Lord to show him who the bride would be:

> Behold, I stand here by the well of wa-
> ter; and the daughters of the men of
> the city come out to draw water: And
> let it come to pass, that the damsel to
> whom I shall say, Let down thy pitcher,
> I pray thee, that I may drink; and she

shall say, Drink, and I will give thy camels drink also: let the same be she that thou hast appointed for thy servant Isaac; and thereby shall I know that thou hast showed kindness unto my master. And it came to pass, before he had done speaking, that, behold, Rebekah came out, who was born to Bethuel, son of Milcah, the wife of Nahor, Abraham's brother, with her pitcher upon her shoulder. And the damsel was very fair to look upon, a virgin, neither had any man known her: and she went down to the well, and filled her pitcher, and came up. And the servant ran to meet her, and said, Let me, I pray thee, drink a little water of thy pitcher. And she said, Drink, my lord: and she hasted, and let down her pitcher upon her hand, and gave him drink. And when she had done giving him drink, she said, I will draw water for thy camels also, until they have done drinking. And she hasted, and emptied her pitcher into the trough, and ran again unto the well to draw water, and drew for all his camels. And the man wondering at her held his peace, to wit whether the LORD had made his journey prosperous or not. (Genesis 24:13–21)

The servant was praying for a divine appointment with Isaac's bride. He had ten camels which had traveled hundreds of miles. The water gauge on these camels was on "E" for empty! It was time to fill up. Eliezer stopped praying. He looked up and saw this damsel, and he ran to her. As she saw him, she offered water not only to Eliezer but also for the camels. It takes about 30 gallons of water to fill up one camel.[2] She may have pulled 300 gallons of water out of the well. Now, that is servanthood!

The bride of Christ is going to be a servant-bride. Notice that Eliezer did not pray that the prospective bride be one that was pretty or talented. He prayed for actions showing that she had an unselfish character which comes with a servant's heart. I believe that what Eliezer prayed was the heart of Abraham. This is also what Jesus has told us to pray. He said in Matthew 9:38, "Pray ye therefore the Lord of the harvest, that he will send forth laborers into his harvest." The key to evangelism is not praying for the lost but praying for laborers for the ripened fields of souls. He is looking for those who will serve Him out of love.

It is interesting that we assume the servant to be Eliezer who is mentioned in Genesis. Chapter 24 does not specifically mention the servant's name, but it is inferred. This is the story of the nameless servant. Eliezer does not receive the credit for bringing home the bride although we can assume that it was him. Someone once said that there is no telling how much could be done in the church if people weren't seeking credit. I think God is going to write another book after Revelation is fulfilled and the world is over. It is going to be God's reflections on world history, and it is going to be called, *Nameless Servants: How the World Was Won.*

God is mobilizing average believers from all ages. The local church is becoming the training and sending base for everyday believers. The superstar mentality is dead. We can appreciate the great crusades, the TV evangelists, and the work they are doing, but the bottom line is that the world is going to be won by nameless bond servants who say, "I love my master, and I will serve him forever by bringing a bride home for his Son."

The call to be the bride of Christ, to be the local church, is a call to endless servanthood. There are some things you never graduate from in the body of Christ, and one of these things is servanthood. We are following someone who said, "For even the Son of man came not to be ministered unto, but to minister, and to give his life a ransom for many" (Mark 10:45). Jesus, who first loved us by giving His life, compels and constrains us to be that servant. We are not to serve just out of duty, but we are to also serve out of love for the One who set us free. Has His love pierced your heart to the extent that you are ready to become the free-will bond servant? Can you say, "I love you, Lord, and I want to bring home a bride for you," and then go and do it?

4

The Relationship of Owner to Steward

And Abraham said unto his eldest servant that ruled over all that he had.
—Genesis 24:2

In Genesis 24:2, we see another aspect of the relationship. It says, "And Abraham said unto his eldest servant of his house that ruled over all that he had." Abraham was owner of it all, yet he entrusted the servant with all that he owned. The Greek word for steward means the manager of a house, and Eliezer was the steward of all that Abraham owned. Jesus is our Lord and owner of our very lives. First, he has the right as owner because He is the creator, and we are His creation. Secondly, Christ is the rightful owner because He has purchased us. The Bible says,

37

> What? know ye not that your body is the temple of the Holy Ghost which is in you, which ye have of God, and ye are not your own? For ye are bought with a price: therefore glorify God in your body, and in your spirit, which are God's. (1 Cor. 6:19–20)

You are not your own! All that you have, all that you are, and all that you ever hope to be, as Dallas Holmes sings, is His. He owns it. Jesus Christ is the rightful owner because He has purchased the rights to our lives through His shed blood. He is your owner because He has redeemed you or bought you back from the devil. You were in the kingdom of darkness, and through His blood you have been purchased and placed into the kingdom of light. He owns us, and we are His stewards. When He purchased us, He invested in us His life, Spirit, grace, power, and ability.

In Genesis 1:28, man was created to rule over every redeemed thing. In Genesis 3, Adam lost that dominion. By sinning, he gave it to Satan. Every man since Adam has also sinned; thus, all have yielded their rights to Satan. Satan is the prince of this lost and sin-filled world. In Matthew 4, Satan came to Jesus and offered Him the kingdoms of the world if He would bow down to him. Jesus never refuted the fact that Satan had the authority to offer the kingdoms because Satan had that authority.

Once we are redeemed in God, we become a second Adam through Jesus Christ. Like the first Adam, we are to take dominion and subdue the earth again. The main means of subduing the earth and gaining dominion is through the preaching of the gospel for the salvation of souls. Jesus invested His life, Spirit, grace, and power to enable us to live and witness. The manifestation of people coming to Christ will result in redeeming cultures and whole societies through the gospel —the good news of Jesus Christ.

Francis Frangipane tells how the unified city-wide church in Cedar Rapids, Iowa, has helped to reduce the crime rate 17 percent by preaching the gospel. We are subduing the earth through the gospel. The history of missions shows how the gospel has transformed people, groups, and nations. The gospel transforms us from poverty to production, from no antidote against lethal diseases to healings (medically and supernaturally), from anarchy to order and peace. Because they are kept and enforced by men, laws do not change governments. People need to be transformed by the power of the gospel before the government will change.

Jesus Christ has invested his life, power, and grace in us as individuals and as the corporate body of Christ. Therefore, he has invested in His kingdom. He has given us the kingdom (Luke 12:32). We, then, are stewards of the kingdom of God. Jesus, in the parable of the unmerciful servant, tells us that there is an accountability in and for his kingdom. Stewardship is the use or oversight of that with which you have been entrusted. We express what our master has deposited in our lives by depositing the kingdom in others. Out of gratitude in our hearts for the king and His everlasting kingdom, we work to establish His dominion in men's hearts.

Jesus gave us the stewardship of the kingdom when he turned it over to the Gentiles (Matt. 21:43). We are called the light and the salt of the earth. We are stewards who are to preserve God's earth by using the penetrating light of the gospel.

Dr. John White wrote a parable about orange pickers. It depicts our responsibility as Christians and the consequences when we do not carry it out:

> I dreamed I drove on a Florida road. It was still and straight and empty. On either side were groves of orange trees....This was harvest time.

My wonder grew as the miles slipped by. How could the harvest be gathered?

But at last, I saw some orange pickers. Far from the highway, almost on the horizon, lost in the vast wilderness of unpicked fruit, I could discern a tiny group of them working steadily. Many miles later, I saw another group. I could not be sure, but I suspected that the earth beneath me was shaking with silent laughter at the hopelessness of their task. Yet, the pickers went on picking.

The sun had long passed its zenith, and the shadows were lengthening as I turned a corner of the road to see a sign that read, "Leaving NEGLECTED COUNTY/Entering HOME COUNTY." The contrast was so startling that I scarcely had time to take in the sign. I had to slow down, for all at once, the traffic was heavy. People by the thousands swarmed the road and crowded the sidewalks.

I parked the car at the roadside, and I mingled with the crowd. Smart gowns, neat shoes, showy hats, expensive suits, and starched shirts made me a little conscious of my own work clothes. Everyone seemed so fresh, poised, and gay.

I made my way further into the trees. Most of the people were carrying a book. Bound beautifully in leather and edged and lettered in gold, the book was entitled, "Orange Picker's Manual."

I noticed around one of the orange trees that seats had been arranged. Just as I got to my seat, everyone stood and began to sing. The man next to me shared his song book with me. It was called, "Songs of the Orange Groves."

After a while, a rather fat man took over from the song leader. After reading two sentences from his well-thumbed copy of the manual, he began to make a speech. I wasn't clear on whether he was addressing the people or the oranges.

"Which trees do we pick from?" I asked the man beside me.

"We don't pick oranges," the man explained. "We haven't been called. That's the Orange Picker's job. We're here to support him. Besides, we haven't been to college. You need to know how an orange thinks before you can pick it successfully—orange psychology, you know. Most of these folks here," he went on, pointing to the congregation, "have never been to Manual School."

"Manual School," I whispered. "What's that?"

42

"It's where they go to study the manual," he said. "It's very hard to understand. You need years of study before it makes sense."

..."We have much to be thankful for. Last week we saw *three* oranges brought into our baskets, and we are not completely debt-free from the money we owed on the cushion covers that grace the seats you now sit on," said the fat man as he was reaching the climax in his speech.

"Do we start on the picking now?" I asked my informant.

"What in the world do you think we're doing?" He hissed. "What do you suppose this tremendous effort has been made for? There's more orange-picking talent in this group than in the rest of Home County. Thousands of dollars have been spent on the tree you're looking at."

I apologized quickly. "I wasn't being critical," I said. "And I'm sure the fat man must be a very good orange picker, but surely, the rest of us could try. After all, there are so many oranges that need picking. We've all got a pair of hands, and we could read the manual."

"When you've been in the business as long as I have, you'll realize that it's not as simple as that," he replied. "There isn't time....We have our work to do, our families to care for, and our homes to look after. We..."

But, I wasn't listening. Light was beginning to break on me. Whatever these people were, they were not orange pickers. Orange picking was just a form of entertainment for their weekends.

...Everywhere the ground was littered with fallen fruit. As I watched, it seemed that before my eyes the trees began to rain oranges. Many of them rotting on the ground....[1]

Souls are rotting away. It is not a dream. We are to care for a world diseased in sin. Each passing day, hundreds of thousands go to the kingdom of darkness forever. Now is the time, and today is the day for all in His kingdom to go to war and win souls. This is why we have become new creatures in Christ.

The apostle Paul felt a personal accountability and sense of stewardship for the gospel and the gifts committed to him, as determined by the following passages:

Whereof I am made a minister, according to the dispensation of God which is given to me for you, to fulfill the word of God.   (Col. 1:25)

But as we were allowed of God to be put in trust with the gospel, even so we speak; not as pleasing men, but God, which trieth our hearts. (1 Thess. 2:4)

For though I preach the gospel, I have nothing to glory of: for necessity is laid upon me; yea, woe is unto me, if I preach not the gospel! (1 Cor. 9:16)

According to the glorious gospel of the blessed God, which was committed to my trust. (1 Tim. 1:11)

But hath in due times manifested his word through preaching, which is committed unto me according to the commandment of God our Savior. (Titus 1:3)

This commandment, which Paul speaks of, is the Great Commission:

Go ye therefore, and teach all nations, baptizing them in the name of the Father, and of the Son, and of the Holy Ghost: Teaching them to observe all things whatsoever I have commanded you: and, lo, I am with you always, even unto the end of the world. Amen. (Matt. 28:19–20)

> And he said unto them, Go ye into all
> the world, and preach the gospel to
> every creature.   (Mark 16:15)

Paul is not alone in this stewardship of
the gospel. In 2 Corinthians 5:17–6:2 we are
given an account that details the salvation we
have in Christ and our responsibility for the
privilege received. 2 Corinthians 5:17 affirms,
"Therefore if any man be in Christ, he is a
new creature: old things are passed away; behold, all things are become new." Paul goes on
to say that we are given the ministry of reconciliation. The apostle is saying that one who
has been reconciled will be a good steward by
ministering reconciliation to others.

If a ministry's ultimate end is not the reconciliation of the lost, it is not a biblical ministry. This is the ministry God has given the
church. We are stewards of the reconciling
blood of Jesus Christ. Jesus, before sending
out His disciples, said, "Freely ye have received, freely give" (Matt. 10:8).

"Now then we are ambassadors for
Christ" (2 Cor. 5:20). An ambassador is a representative of a country or kingdom, and this
representative's responsibilities are to protect
the territory and advance it against others.
Having been invested with kingdom riches, we
are now accountable to promote the interest

46

of the kingdom that has been given. Thus, we must bring home a bride for the Prince of Peace.

Lastly, in 2 Corinthians 5:21, Paul relates that Christ, being without sin, took on our sin and made us, who are unrighteous, righteous (right before God). Second Corinthians 6:1 then refers to those who have received the righteousness of Christ. It says, "We then, as workers together with him, beseech you also that ye receive not the grace of God in vain." You, who have been made righteous, receive not the grace of God in vain, but become channels of that grace to save others. Paul is challenging the church not to waste the power and ability given to us to declare the kingdom of God. Therefore, preach God's rule on the earth while men and women still have time to be saved.

"Blessed are the poor in spirit, for theirs is the kingdom of heaven" (Matt. 5:3), says the first Beatitude. I discovered the word *poor* literally means "to have no source of income." My mind pictured the panhandlers and homeless in the streets of America and those worse off on the city streets of Nigeria who have only patches of old clothes or none at all.

I realize that, before God, this is what I am like apart from Christ. Without Christ, my

47

righteousness is as a filthy beggar's rags. Yet, God gives to beggars his royal robe of righteousness. We go from beggars to princes in the kingdom of God.

I like the World Missionary Press tract entitled, "Who Am I That a King Would Die For Me?" A king dying for beggars—unthinkable. A king giving beggars the authority to rule in his kingdom—not possible. But, it happened, and you and I are the proof.

Our witness to the world is a stewardship of the riches that the King has graciously bestowed upon us through His death. Our proclamation of the gospel is our means of expressing appreciation for the King who died for us.

5

The Relationship of Covenant Partner/ Friend to Friend

And Abraham said unto his eldest servant of his house, that ruled over all that he had, Put, I pray thee, thy hand under my thigh.
—*Genesis 24:2*

The master and the servant had a covenant partner relationship. Abraham and Eliezer made an agreement or *covenant* together. Keil and Delitzcsh's *Commentary on the Old Testament* says, "Abraham made the servant take an oath in order that his wishes might be inviolably fulfilled, even if he himself should die in the interim."[1] Regardless of death, this covenant was to be fulfilled. Abraham binds the servant in obligation by having him take an oath of covenant. In making this covenant, Abraham says, in effect, "Servant, I want you to swear that if I die in the process of your getting a bride for Isaac, you will finish the job. If I never see you again, Servant, I want you to swear that you will bring home a bride for my son."

The act of putting a hand underneath the thigh of the one with whom you are making the covenant is also found in Genesis 47:29. In this passage, Jacob tells Joseph to put his hand underneath his thigh and to swear that his bones would not be left in Egypt but taken to the land that was promised. This is significant because it represents an idea of posterity. It is for all descendants of all generations. By making a like covenant, Eliezer commits not only himself but all of his children's children. It was a commitment to preserve the lineage of Abraham.

We are covenant partners with God under a blood covenant through Jesus Christ. All those who come under this blood covenant become obligated to carry out the last wish of the Lord. "Go ye therefore, and teach all nations, baptizing them in the name of the Father, and of the Son, and of the Holy Ghost" (Matt. 28:19). We are in effect saying under covenant, "Yes, Lord and my children's children will, too."

In Genesis 15, Abraham asked God, "How will I know this thing (the promise of inheriting a great land and being the father of many nations) will come to pass?" (Genesis 15:8). In order to assure Abraham, God made an unalterable covenant establishing His will for him and his descendants. Abraham was told to get a three-year-old heifer. Abraham cut the heifer in half and laid the pieces side by side. Abraham then was to walk through the pieces to make a vow to God. However, later the Scripture states, "And it came to pass, that, when the sun went down, and it was dark, behold a smoking furnace, and a burning lamp that passed between those pieces. And the same day the LORD made a covenant with Abra[ha]m" (Gen. 15:17–18).

Did Abraham pass through the pieces? No, a smoky furnace and a burning lamp did. The Bible calls the Lord "a wall of fire" (Zech. 2:5). It was the Lord who passed through the pieces and made a vow to Abraham, thus cutting a covenant with him.

God reaches down to man and makes covenant with him. Just as Abraham did not make covenant with God, neither can we. Jesus made a blood covenant with us when His body was cut and torn for our sins. It was a covenant we could never be able to establish. Howver, our Lord and Savior passed through this suffering to make us benefactors of His unalterable will.

Jesus made a covenant, and He established His will on earth. What is His will? His will is that all would come to repentance, and none would perish. The Lord says that He will put His laws in our hearts and write them on our minds. Plus, He will not remember our sins and iniquities any more (Hebrews 10:17).

We can share this covenant, cut by Christ, with others. This is our obligation. Paul tells us in Romans 1:14–16:

> I am debtor both to the Greeks, and to the Barbarians; both to the wise, and to the unwise. So, as much as in me is, I am ready to preach the gospel to you that are at Rome also. For I am not ashamed of the gospel of Christ: for it is the power of God unto salvation to every one that believeth; to the Jew first, and also to the Greek.

Paul was under obligation and says in Acts 20:26–27:

> Wherefore I take you to record this day, that I am pure from the blood of all men. For I have not shunned to declare unto you all the counsel of God.

We should all be able to stand before God and say, "I am innocent of the blood of all men because I have not failed to share the full testament of God." The Lord's Supper affirms the blood covenant between the Redeemer and His redeemed. As we are participating in this memorial, we are saying, "Jesus, You have delivered me. I am in Your new and living way. Jesus, your will (of souls being saved) is still in effect, and I am committed to proclaiming Your death and resurrection until you return."

Paul, in Romans 10, reminds the believers in Rome that they should be responsible with the blessing of salvation. In Romans 10:14 Paul asks four questions:

- How then shall they call on him in whom they have not believed?
- How shall they believe in him of whom they have not heard?
- How shall they hear without a preacher?
- How shall they preach, except they be sent?

Four good questions! Are you fulfilling the blood covenant by giving to world missions? Faith comes by hearing the Word of God. How will they hear unless someone preaches? Are you preaching and testifying? Is your home open for ministry? Are you involved in encouraging and training new believers? (They are the next generation to be sent.)

When I think of the blood covenant, I think of those who were willing to suffer and die because of it. Their blood has preserved the faith and given us the opportunity to hear and be saved. As Tertalian, a church Patriarch, said, "the blood of the martyrs is the seed of the church."[2]

It has been said, "Tell me how much you have suffered, and I will then tell you how much you have loved." So that those for whom Christ died can receive His life-giving gospel, how much have you sacrificed, shared and suffered? To what degree have you done any of these for your covenant partner? Jesus challenged his disciples with this verse, "Greater love hath no man than this, that a man lay down his life for his friends" (John 15:13). The word *friend*, literally means "covenant partner." Abraham and Eliezer were friends in covenant. Jesus was a friend to us in that he laid down his life for us.

Jesus is also a brother to us. Hebrews 2:11 says that He and the sanctified are one, and therefore, he is not ashamed to call us His brethren. Our friend and brother Jesus in effect makes this request of us, "Friend, will you bring back my bride for me?" That is what Abraham said to the servant. As one friend to another friend, Abraham, in effect, appeals to Eliezer, "Friend, will you bring home a wife for my son?" That is a friendship covenant.

In 1 Samuel 18, David and Jonathan made a friendship covenant by exchanging oaths, clothing and weapons. They made a covenant forever between their families. This is the kind of relationship that we have with Jesus Christ. Jesus has exchanged His clothing with us. We exchanged our righteousness which was as filthy rags (Isa. 64:6) and have been given His robe of righteousness:

> For He hath made Him to be sin for us, who knew no sin; that we might be made the righteousness of God in Him. (2 Cor. 5:21)

David and Jonathan's exchanging of swords represents the taking on of each other's enemies. We are going to take on the Lord's enemies, and He is going to take on our enemies. We have common foes: Satan and his demons. The Bible tells us that Jesus came to destroy the works of the devil (the works of our enemy). Spiritual warfare is not an option. We are called to fight the good fight. We are called to endure hardships as good soldiers.

We overcome by loving Jesus, not our own lives, even unto death.

David and Jonathan said that their covenant would be forever. This meant that they would look after each other's descendants. After Jonathan died and David became king, this actually took place. David asked, "Is there not any of the house of Saul [Jonathan's descendants] that I may show the kindness of God to him?" (2 Sam. 9:3). Mephibosheth, Jonathan's lame son, was brought before David and given all the lands owned by his father Jonathan and grandfather Saul. Then, David declared that Mephibosheth would always eat bread at the king's table (2 Sam. 9:10).

This is symbolic of the believer's covenant with God today. God, like David, promises to take care of us and our descendants. One day, we will inherit the earth and sup at heaven's banquet table. As God takes care of our son's sons, we also are in covenant to see that God's lineage continues throughout time on earth. His kingdom has no end. We do this by bringing home the bride.

James 2:21 continues the concept of covenant partner or friend by saying, "Was not Abraham our father justified by works, when he had offered Isaac his son upon the altar?" This Scripture is saying that Abraham was a friend of God by what he did. That is what

Jesus says in John 14:15, "If ye love me, keep my commandments." How do you know if you are a friend to Jesus? He says, "Ye are my friends, if ye do whatsoever I command you" (John 15:14).

The demonstration of being in covenant with the Son is the obedience to His commands. Jesus has been a faithful friend. Show yourself to be His faithful friend by doing His will. That is the relationship of a covenant partner.

The Relationship of Father to Son

And Abraham said, Behold, to me thou has
given no seed:
and, lo, one born in mine house is mine heir.
—Genesis 15:3

The last aspect of the relationship between Abraham and the servant was father to son. Specifically for us, it is Father to adopted son. It says in Genesis 15:1–3:

> After these things the word of the LORD came unto Abram in a vision, saying, Fear not, Abram: I am thy shield, and thy exceeding great reward. And Abram said, Lord GOD, what wilt thou give me, seeing I go childless, and the steward of my house is this Eliezer of Damascus? And Abram said, Behold, to me thou hast given no seed: and, lo, one born in my house is mine heir.

Abraham is complaining of being childless. Eliezer was likely to be the sole heir and heir to the promise. You could paraphrase this by saying, "This servant is like a son to me. Am I to adopt him so that he might be heir to the promise and all that I have?" God quickly reaffirms that the promise of a son is not in a figurative sense, but it is to be fulfilled literally. Then, God and Abraham make a covenant.

Abraham's consideration of the adoption of Eliezer tells us something about the relationship that they had. Eliezer, though a servant, was like a son, so why not adopt him? Eliezer was not the son of promise, but he was a son—an adopted son.

Abraham appealed to Eliezer as an adopted son when he asked him to get Isaac a bride. Eliezer desired nothing more than to be a servant. Out of gratitude and love for the father, Eliezer gladly took on the mission.

The servant's relationship to Abraham is similar to our relationship with the Father. Jesus illustrated the relationship with his parable of the prodigal son in Luke 15. The prodigal son rehearsed what he was going to say to his father:

> I will arise and go to my father, and will say unto him, Father, I have sinned against heaven, and before thee,

And am no more worthy to be called
thy son: make me as one of thy hired
servants.   (Luke 15:18–19)

This is how we go to God the Father. We
go to Him saying, "Father, I am not worthy to
be your son. Only make me a servant." Servants we are, but God calls us to be more. Even
though we are servants, He calls us sons.

The TV show *The Crusaders* covers human interest stories of people who are doing
or have done courageous things. One particular program focused on the Williams family.
Pat Williams is the General Manager of the
Orlando Magic, a professional basketball team
in Florida. The Williams' have four children of
their own, yet Pat's wife wanted to adopt
more children. They started adopting children
—all street kids from different countries.
They eventually adopted twenty. *The Crusaders* filmed the family of twenty-six at work.

In order for this family to function or-
derly, everyone had to work together. Each
person had specific tasks and was happy to
complete them. This job system began with
the first few adopted children. In order for
them to continue to expand their family, each
member had to have responsibilities. They
had to serve. Their smiles and joy were not
camera-ready but genuine.

If I were a street kid from Brazil, Korea, or somewhere else, I would be happy to be an adopted son or daughter of Pat Williams. Not only is he a rich American, but he is a God-fearing man. Through Jesus Christ we are adopted into God's royal family of believers. God desires to be the Father of every last soul on earth. Like the Williams' children, our responsible actions will help others to come into God's adopted family.

There are many Scriptures that depict us as children or sons of God. Two such verses are from Romans and Galatians:

> For as many as are led by the Spirit of God, they are the sons of God. For ye have not received the spirit of bondage again to fear; but ye have received the Spirit of adoption, whereby we cry, Abba, Father. The Spirit itself beareth witness with our spirit, that we are the children of God: And if children, then heirs; heirs of God, and joint-heirs with Christ; if so be that we suffer with him, that we may be also glorified together.
> (Romans 8:14–17)

> But when the fulness of the time was come, God sent forth his Son, made of a woman, made under the law, To redeem them that were under the law,

that we might receive the adoption of sons. And because ye are sons, God hath sent forth the Spirit of his Son into your hearts, crying, Abba, Father. Wherefore thou art no more a servant, but a son; and if a son, then an heir of God through Christ. (Galatians 4:4–7)

Although we are not the Son, we are adopted by the Father through the blood of Jesus. Having been regenerated by the Holy Spirit, we become sons of God and co-heirs with Christ. And now we can cry, "Abba Father," which means "Daddy." These verses reveal the intimacy that we have in our relationship with the Father through Jesus.

Out of this intimacy, God the Father appeals to us as adopted sons asking, "Will you bring home a bride for the Son of Promise?" God says, "I am going to call you my son." We do not deserve to be called sons, merely servants. Yet, as sons we come to know the heart desires of the Father and Son, and through the power of the Holy Spirit, we begin to fulfill those desires.

As a young boy in Argentina, the founder of Harvest Evangelism, Ed Silvoso was made to take afternoon naps. He had some difficulty settling down in the middle of the afternoon, so his father would nap with him. Whenever he saw his father's eyes closed, Ed was gripped by a fear of death. His was afraid of losing his parents because they had lost theirs in childhood. Ed would lean his ear to his father's chest. After hearing his heartbeat, his fears were put to rest. Ed would even put lyrics to his father's pumping heart. "I love you, son. I will not die."

Relating his experience to the church's need to hear the heartbeat of God, he encourages us by saying that we should lean our ears on God's chest. He says to listen to His heartbeat until we see all of our unsaved friends, relatives, coworkers, and neighbors in the monitor of our souls. As their names and faces appear, we are to listen to God and say, "None should perish but all come to repentance." [1]

Jesus is our example. As a Son, he sought to fulfill the desires of the Father. He came to seek and save the lost. He was anointed to set the captives free. He absolutely obeyed the voice and desire of the Father:

> Then answered Jesus and said unto them, Verily, verily, I say unto you, The Son can do nothing of himself, but what he seeth the Father do: for what things soever he doeth, these also doeth the Son likewise. For the Father loveth the Son, and showeth him all things

that himself doeth: and he will show
him greater works than these, that ye
may marvel. For as the Father raiseth
up the dead, and quickeneth them;
even so the Son quickeneth whom he
will.   (John 5:19–21)

We are to walk as Jesus did—unto the Father.
In Acts 10:38, Peter says,

God anointed Jesus of Nazareth with
the Holy Ghost and with power: who
went about doing good, and healing all
that were oppressed of the devil; for
God was with him.

He did these things by the Holy Spirit,
and this is how we know we are the sons of
God. Romans 8:14 says, "For as many as are
led by the Spirit of God, they are the sons of
God." God brings the Holy Spirit into our
lives to instruct us in the ways that we should
go. Notice that Abraham instructs the servant
in the way that he should go. The servant says,

And I bowed down my head, and worshipped the LORD, and blessed the LORD
God of my master Abraham, which had
led me in the right way to take my
master's brother's daughter unto his
son.   (Genesis 24:48)

God will show you the way because it is the heart of God to bring home a bride for His Son. If you are led by God, you will always have an open door for witnessing. It is not always a situation where you have to speak, but it will be a witnessing situation. We know this because the work of the Holy Spirit is to glorify or testify of the Father and the Son. Who is He going to use to glorify the Father and Son? Us!

The evangelism of Jesus was to reveal the Father to the people. Jesus was concerned about the image of God. The Pharisees and Sadducees were placing rules on the people that they could not bear (concerning the Sabbath day and ceremonial washings). These rules gave the people the impression that God was oppressive and a hard taskmaster. Jesus was upset because He knew these practices neither glorified nor revealed the Father as He is. Therefore, to make a statement, Jesus would purposely heal on the Sabbath. By his actions, Jesus was telling the people that the things the Pharisees and Sadducees were saying about God the Father were not portraying an accurate or true image. Jesus promoted God as a loving, benevolent Father. Jesus said:

> If a son shall ask bread of any of you that is a father, will he give him a stone? or if he ask a fish, will he for a

fish give him a serpent? Or if he shall ask an egg, will he offer him a scorpion? If ye then, being evil, know how to give good gifts unto your children: how much more shall your heavenly Father give the Holy Spirit to them that ask him? (Luke 11:11–13)

Robert Stein writes about Jesus' frequent and unique address of God as "Abba." He says that Jesus addresses God the Father in a way that denotes warmth and tenderness not found elsewhere.[2]

It is no wonder that crowds were drawn to Jesus. The love-starved Jews, having only known God as cold and aloof, flocked to know God as "Abba Father." Our love-deficient society needs to know God as Father. A fatherless generation desperately needs to know a Father who cares for, comforts, and disciplines those He loves. "It is a grand privilege and calling for those who know God as their Father to graciously invite unbelievers to meet God as their Father and not as Judge."[3] They need to see a Father who loves His children equally. They need to observe His children coming from every stream of life and being united by His love. Punkers, Bikers, Rednecks, Hispanics, Asians, Africans, sinners, and the once religious, self-righteous need to come together to love each other and their "Daddy" who gave them birth.

In our one parent generation, the invitation to know God as a faithful Father is attractive. The only ones who can reveal God, as a Father to a fatherless world, are His children. Therefore, evangelism is the family business. The boy Jesus said, "Wist ye not that I must be about my Father's business?" (Luke 2:49). I believe Jesus at age 12 was doing more than probing religious minds that day in the temple. I believe that He was evangelizing the religious leaders of His day. Even then, He was trying to teach them of God as Father.

Bringing home the bride is the business of the family, and the job of the family is to propagate more family. It is the business of the family, for the family, and by the family:

> And another of his disciples said unto him, Lord, suffer me first to go and bury my father. But Jesus said unto him, Follow me; and let the dead bury their dead. And when he was entered into a ship, his disciples followed him.
> (Matt. 8:21–23)

Jesus was not being insensitive to the son's need to honor his father. He was saying that "there are certain things which the spiritually dead can do just as well as believers, but there are other things in life that only the believer can do. Let the spiritually dead bury the physically dead. But as for you, be indispensable. Let the main thrust be to advance His cause on earth."[4]

There are certain things that only family members can do! Family members are the only people qualified to evangelize. We alone are qualified because we are the only ones who know Him as Father.

Evangelist Leighton Ford's daughter was lost, and he began to search for her in every conceivable place. As time passed, he said,

> I came to an overwhelming sense that my daughter was lost. Nothing seemed important. Every other plan I had for the day was discarded. I went up and down searching every street, alley and corner with one intense, urgent desire: to find my daughter.[5]

This is what God feels for his lost creation. No one else can feel the overwhelming, intense desire that God feels for His lost children; no one but you, His family members.

We are unworthy to be His sons, for we are only servants. Yet, He graciously and mercifully adopts us as sons and daughters, heirs to His kingdom, co-heirs to His throne. In effect, He asks, "Will you go get a bride for my Son of Promise, Jesus Christ?"

You are the only ones who know what it is like to be a family member. You alone can express the Father's desire to a fatherless world. The Beatitude, "Blessed are the peacemakers for they shall be called the children of God" (Matt. 5:9), will be spoken of you.

7

Our Camels Are Loaded to Attract

And the servant took ten camels of the camels of his master, and departed; for all the goods of his master were in his hand.
—Genesis 24:10

Abraham loaded ten camels. The number ten represents completeness, and the loading of the camels represents God the Father loading down the church with all that is needed to bring home a bride for the bridegroom, Jesus.

The main asset we have been given is Himself in and through the Holy Spirit. In the Book of Acts, Peter refers to an Old Testament prophecy that is found in Joel 2:28:

And it shall come to pass in the last days, saith God, I will pour out of my Spirit upon all flesh: and your sons and your daughters shall prophesy, and your young men shall see visions, and your old men shall dream dreams.

(Acts 2:17)

Jesus knew the disciples needed their camels (lives) loaded before starting the church:

But ye shall receive power, after that the Holy Ghost is come upon you: and ye shall be witnesses unto me both in Jerusalem, and in all Judea, and in Samaria, and unto the uttermost part of the earth. (Acts 1:8)

God has equipped us with the Equipper. The job of the Holy Spirit is to equip us so that our lives will reflect the life of our Master, Jesus. The Equipper is equipping us in two areas: in the fruits of the Spirit or Christ-like character and in the gifts of the Holy Spirit and Christ-like service.

Christ-like character has the power to attract the lost to our beautiful Savior. In the Beatitudes, Jesus said, "Blessed are..." He did not say, *Blessed was* or *Blessed will be*, but *"Blessed are."* Jesus emphasized your *being* because what you are affects what you do. The result of beatitude living is found in Matthew 5:13–16:

> Ye are the salt of the earth: but if the salt have lost his savor, wherewith shall it be salted? it is thenceforth good for nothing, but to be cast out, and to be trodden under foot of men. Ye are the light of the world. A city that is set on an hill cannot be hid. Neither do men light a candle, and put it under a bushel, but on a candlestick; and it giveth light unto all that are in the house. Let your light so shine before men, that they may see your good works, and glorify your Father which is in heaven.

If you are all these *blesseds*, then the by-product is that you are salt and light; salt to a perishing world that needs to be preserved and light to a misguided generation in darkness. You are going to have influence and impact in the world through Christ-like character.

When I attended First Christian Church in Clearwater, Florida, I was 22 years old. The thing that impacted me most was seeing the love and joy of the people who were there. I saw husbands loving their wives and kids who enjoyed going to church. I knew, within my sinful life, that they had something that I did not have. They were something that I was not, and this *something* caused me to gravitate their way. My father-in-law once told me, "You can bring a horse to water, but you can't make him drink, although you can make him thirsty." I believe that God has loaded us with His Spirit so that the character of Christ will be lived out through us, making people thirsty for a life in God.

Sheldon Vanauken said, "The best argument for Christianity is Christians with their joy, their certainty, and their completeness. But the strongest argument against Christianity is also Christians, when they are sober and joyless, self-righteous and smug in complacent consecration, narrow and repressive. Then Christianity dies a thousand deaths."[1]

Once, I took my wife and my five children to a Pancho's restaurant. We were going about the routine of eating out when an elderly Hispanic woman approached. "You have such beautiful children," she complimented. I quickly replied, "Thank you," thinking that she was referring to their facial features, but she specified that what was beautiful about them was their obedience. This is a compliment of compliments! Physical beauty is a gift of birth, but inward beauty is developed. The beauty that this woman saw was developed as my wife and I (mostly my wife) worked with the grace of the Holy Spirit.

When my wife and I got married, nearly everyone had come to see her. You could hear the people chatting, "What kind of dress will she wear?" As my wife started down the aisle, teary-eyed women said, "She's a beautiful bride." The point is that the bride is attractive.

When we see a bride who is white, pure, and spotless, she is attractive. The church as the bride of Christ is attractive. The method of the Holy Spirit is one of attraction. The holiness and love of Christ's church brings the unbelievers toward her. The bride with all its body parts flowing and beautifully functioning is like the body of Christ ministering by the fruits and gifts of the Spirit of God. As the church, we are to be the beautiful, powerful, and efficiently functioning body of Christ. A supernatural body that excels as it performs its functions is attractive.

Often unbeknownst to us, the world is watching our character. It can be beautifully attractive which can cause the lost to be enamored with the person of Jesus Christ. Our loveliness is not merely ornamental.

The servant goes on to Mesopotamia, stops at the well, and prays that the girl to be Isaac's bride will come to draw water, giving both himself and his camels a drink. The girl,

Rebekah, was selected to be the bride because of her deeds. The bride of Christ will be known for who she is and for the deeds she does. She will not be known because of how much she knows. We, as the bride of Christ, will not be known by doctrine but by what we are and what we do.

The servant gives Rebekah bracelets and earrings. When you become a part of the bride of Christ, you are bestowed with fruits, gifts, and the ability to bear the fruit of a Christ-like life.

The effectiveness that the fruits and gifts of the Spirit can have on an unbeliever is exemplified in Genesis 24:28–31:

> And the damsel ran, and told them of her mother's house these things. And Rebekah had a brother, and his name was Laban: and Laban ran out unto the man, unto the well. And it came to pass, when he saw the earring and bracelets upon his sister's hands, and when he heard the words of Rebekah his sister, saying, Thus spake the man unto me; that he came unto the man; and, behold, he stood by the camels at the well. And he said, 'Come in, thou blessed of the LORD; wherefore standest thou without? for I have prepared the house, and room for the camels.

Notice what happens here. Worldly, carnal Laban sees his sister and all the gifts. He is drawn to the gifts. Laban is bug-eyed when his sister enters with ears that sparkle. Laban saw, heard, and then ran to see this man of God.

In the book of Acts, we see that this is exactly how evangelism was done. Pagan idol worshippers, worldly philosophers, and wretched sinners saw the miracles. They saw the life of the believers, heard the message, and were converted. That is how it happened then and still happens today! People are going to see, then hear and be converted! Remember, Christianity is what we as Christians can do that unbelievers cannot do. John 1:12 says, "But as many as received him, to them gave he power to become the sons of God, even to them that believe on his name." Anyone can go to church. I can get a monkey to go to church and sit, but to live the Christian life takes the power of God. This is the attraction method of evangelism.

Christ-like service, along with the gifts of the Holy Spirit, is also effective in drawing others to Christ. *Charisma* magazine tells of Pastor Steve Sjogren and his twenty-eight-hundred member Vineyard Fellowship in Cincinnati, Ohio, who are working on a program called Conspiracy of Kindness. His church evangelizes through kindness. For example, his members go into restaurants and ask to clean the toilet. The owners ask, "What are you going to charge?" "Oh, nothing, we just want to demonstrate a practical love for you," they say. They do many other acts of kindness and charity because that is what is in their hearts. The pastor said that many people visit his church after they encounter such acts of kindness. "People don't necessarily remember what they are told of God's love, but they never forget what they have experienced of God's love," he says.[2]

Matthew 5:16 says, "Let your light so shine before men, that they may see your good works, and glorify your Father which is in heaven." Shining our light is equivalent to doing good deeds. Therefore, to lack good deeds is to have a dimmed light like one hiding under a bushel. As James says, without works our faith is dead.

In a book on missions by Ruth Tucker, *From Jerusalem to Iran Jaya*, she explains the spread of Christianity throughout the whole Roman Empire. She entitled the first 400 years of Christianity, "The Irresistible Advance."[3] I like that! Christ has loaded us with His Spirit so that we might lift up Jesus and bring on this irresistible advance. Jesus is irresistible, and if we reflect Him in character, others will be drawn. That is why the cleaning of toilets by the Vineyard Church in Cincinnati is such an irresistible act of love.

In Genesis 45, Pharaoh learned of Joseph's brothers. Pharaoh told Joseph to bring his father and households, and they would be given the good land of Egypt. Joseph built them wagons according to the commandment of Pharaoh and gave them provisions for their travel. Joseph sent out his brothers, and they departed. They went up out of Egypt, came to the land of Canaan and to Jacob their father, and told him that Joseph was still alive and was ruler over all the land in Egypt. Jacob was stunned, and he did not believe them. When they told him what Joseph had spoken to them and he *saw* the wagons that Joseph had sent to carry him, Jacob's spirit was revived. "And Israel said, It is enough; Joseph my son is yet alive: I will go and see him before I die" (Genesis 45:28).

Joseph forgave his brothers and brought them before Pharaoh, who told them not to worry about their things because all the goods of Egypt were at their disposal. Pharaoh loaded them down. Likewise, God the Father provides for us like Pharaoh promised to provide for Jacob's family. Jesus says in Luke 12:32, "Fear not, little flock; for it is your Father's good pleasure to give you the kingdom."

Jacob could not believe that Joseph was still alive until he saw the donkeys and wagons that were loaded down. In the same way, many people do not believe that Jesus is alive until they see the miraculous working in a believer who has been loaded down with spiritual gifts.

Like the brothers who betrayed Joseph, we betrayed Jesus. We crucified Him with our sins. We come to Him in our time of famine and say, "God, my life is a mess. Will you have mercy on me?" God responds to us through Jesus, just as Joseph responded to his guilty brothers who sought mercy. Genesis 50:20 records the famous reply of Joseph:

> But as for you, ye thought evil against me; but God meant it unto good, to bring to pass, as it is this day, to save much people alive.

Jesus our brother, whom we betrayed, responds to us in the same way. Not holding our sins against us, He forgives and empowers us. He gives us a job to do and then loads us down with kingdom gifts and power to do kingdom work. As we go out with our wagons loaded to unbelieving people in famine, they will respond to the fruit and gifts of God displayed in us. When they see our camels loaded down, their eyes will be opened, and they will believe the message that Jesus Christ is alive and is reigning as King.

Joseph was not only alive, but he was on the throne. Jacob saw the gifts that Joseph had given to his brothers, then he believed that his son was alive. Laban saw the gifts that the servant had given to Rebekah, then he was open to hear. In the New Testament, unbelievers first saw the miraculous gifts of the Holy Spirit, then they believed.

As we, the church, become arrayed in Christ-like attire, we are ready for war. Our beauty is for battle.

In Song of Solomon, the lover describes his bride:

> Who is she that looketh forth as the morning, fair as the moon, clear as the sun, and terrible as an army with banners? (Song of Sol. 6:10)

The bride's beauty is viewed as an invincible army by her lover. This metaphor describes the reality of the power in the beauty of a Christ-like individual and church. "The weapons of our warfare are not carnal, but mighty through God" (2 Cor. 10:4). We war not as the world. We war through Christ's character. He is our righteousness, and in

81

Him alone is the victory. His presence dispels the presence of the enemy, Satan, who trembles before those who know Jesus.

Thus, our attractiveness as children of light becomes an attack on the kingdom of darkness. Therefore, as we put on Christ, we are loaded to attack as well as attract. Our attraction is an attack on the devil's hold on mankind. One strategy of Satan is to get God's creation in his likeness. He is a liar, deceiver, perverter, and hater of good. He is prideful, jealous, and envious of God. Satan's ploy is to cause us to be like him, and the majority of the world obliges.

Every confrontation that Jesus had with Satan and his devils during his earthly ministry was a blowout. The battle was over about as soon as it began. What our archenemy hates the most is to see Christ formed in you. Against God, he cannot stand. As Christ said, "Hereafter I will not talk much with you: for the prince of this world cometh, and hath nothing in me." In other words, Christ is saying that Satan has tempted Him to sin, but he cannot get through.

When we walk as our Savior walked, we mount an invincible "**attract attack**." The church and individual members make an "attract attack" by being like Christ in character. Thus, attracting the unbeliever becomes an attack on the enemy. How much more the attack when not only godly character but also the power of the Spirit is involved as we minister to the lost. We have brought out the heavy artillery. Backed with the fruits of the spirit, the gifts of the Spirit are an attraction that totally obliterates the effects of Satan. Therefore, the motivation for desiring spiritual gifts is so that you will be more completely conformed to the person and work of our Savior.

In 2 Timothy 2:20–21 we read the following:

> But in a great house there are not only vessels of gold and of silver, but also of wood and of earth; and some to honour, and some to dishonor. If a man therefore purge himself from these, he shall be a vessel unto honor, sanctified, and meet for the master's use, and prepared unto every good work.

If you cleanse your life, you will be what? You will be employable by God and prepared for every good work. A cleansed and righteous life is employable by God. Therefore, we should expect the enduement of the Holy Spirit which makes us employable to minister the gospel. Knowing we have His support gives us confidence to share the gospel. Jesus is our example. In Matthew 6, the multitude was in awe of Christ's teaching because He did not teach as the Pharisees did. He taught as one with authority. He taught not by quoting others but from His own experience. He had walked by the Holy Spirit, and he lived by the Word of God. Therefore, when He spoke, it was with authority, and those who heard were awed by the power.

Those who bear the fruit of Christ-likeness should expect to be strong witnesses because the enduement and authority will accompany them. We should expect Him to load our camels with character traits such as boldness, faith, and courage to preach the gospel. You might say, "Well, I do not have enough boldness." Reach back to camel number three and pull out boldness. If I need faith, I can pull it from camel number two. "I can do all things through Christ which strengtheneth me" (Phil. 4:13). For whatever it is you need, God has loaded your camels. It is there for the asking. So, we are without excuse to bring home a bride for Jesus. We need to go out in faith. We need to believe that whatever any particular person is going to need, God is going to supply.

Agree with God today. Pray this prayer of supplication and thanksgiving:

Lord,

I thank you for loading down my camels. I have everything I need for life and godliness. By you, Holy Spirit, I am a partaker of Your divine nature. So, let others see Your beauty through me and be saved. Lord, let my light shine daily through good deeds so that men will glorify the Father who is in heaven. In Christ's name I pray, Amen.

8

Identifying Your Equipment

And there are diversities of operations, but it is the same God which worketh all in all.
—1 Corinthians 12:6

J esus said, "But if I with the finger of God cast out devils, no doubt the kingdom of God is come upon you" (Luke 11:20). Jesus was demonstrating that His power proves He is the King of the kingdom. When we are operating in the spiritual gifts, we are showing people that the kingdom of God has come upon them. They are in the King's presence. Today, we demonstrate that not only is Jesus alive, but He is also on His throne.

Doctrinally, my religious background did not allow for instantaneous, supernatural healings to take place. As a missionary in

Nigeria, I found that the healings were coming from many supernatural sources, but they were not divine. The Nigerians would put their faith in whatever healed them. These people did not have Medicaid or health care insurance. Often it was, "Be healed or die."

After successfully preaching at the Okpara Inland Village Crusade, I was counseling about thirty young men who had already confessed Christ as Lord or were interested in becoming Christians. I asked them if I could pray for them. One young man asked, "Will you pray for my friend?"

"Well, certainly," I replied. "Where is he?" The small crowd parted, and in the back, being held up by two others, was a young lame man. The friend had put him on his bicycle and biked him to the crusade grounds. They heard that a man of God from the U.S. had come, and they wanted to receive prayer.

I asked hesitantly if he could walk "He can't walk, and he can't hear out of his left ear," said the friend.

I thought, Oh, God, if you ever did a miracle, do one now. The faith of some thirty boys was in the balance. What could I do or say? "I'm sorry, but God doesn't do healings anymore," or, "My doctrine doesn't allow for this?" A God of compassion wanted me to pray for this young man. I prayed for his ears. I smothered the good ear with my hand and asked him if he could hear. He said, "Yes."

I don't know if his faith increased, but mine sure did. I knelt down to pray for his dangling legs. I looked up and asked, "If God heals you, will you take the message of salvation in Jesus Christ wherever you go?"

Again, he heard and said, "Yes."

"God, this young man needs your healing touch," I petitioned. "He has promised that he will take your gospel wherever he goes with these healed legs. Lord, I ask that you heal him now so that all these men might believe."

I did not cast or blast out demons. I did not name it or claim it. I prayed while holding his legs, and I could feel movement like his ligaments and bones coming together. Excitedly, I stood and asked, "Did God heal you?"

"Yes!" he exclaimed.

"Then, walk." He awkwardly took strides to the crusade platform and back.

Immediately, I was rushed by several hundred people. Barren women and men with cataracts were reaching up and asking me to touch them. I understood how Jesus felt as the multitudes sandwiched Him. I prayed for those afflicted with sickness and disease, and I did not leave for several hours. The outreach was extended for another night, and many put their faith in Jesus.

I do not move in the gift of healing as a rule, but God used my prayer of faith that night and on occasion since then. The point is that the gift brought people to believe the message of Jesus Christ. The Holy Spirit's power is attractive. He attracts the lost to the Lord Jesus Christ when His gifts are utilized.

Now, it is by His grace that we reflect Jesus Christ in our character. It is by His grace, meaning His ability, that we can live that life. But, it does not mean an absence of work. We labor for fruit. However, gifts are just that —gifts. You can develop the gift, but you cannot do anything to get it.

It is like the difference between a fruit tree and a Christmas tree. A Christmas tree just receives the gifts, but the fruit tree has to work in order to produce. Just as for the farmer, labor must come before harvest. He is going to plant, water, and plow. We must do the same thing in Christ as we labor for the fruit. We must plow up the fallow, stony heart. We are going to plant the good seed of the Word of God. We will water it with prayer in the Holy Spirit. It will take a painful weeding out of the sinful life. It is going to take labor through His Spirit. When the fruit of Christ is produced in us, it will result in a harvest of souls. There will be an addition of souls as we put off the old man and put on

Christ because this makes us more usable to the Master.

By God's grace, we have been given spiritual gifts to be successful in Christian living. God has determined that the success of His church comes through Christians using their specific gifts in unity. Gift projection and the push for uniformity of gifts stifles God's formula for success in the church. God has arranged the parts of the body, every one of them, just as He wanted them to be (1 Cor. 12:6).

Dizzy Dean, a great baseball pitcher, probably never thought that his baseball career would depend upon his big toe. While pitching in the World Series, a batter hit a line drive. The ball ricocheted off of Dizzy's big toe and broke it. The toe failed to mend properly. As a result, he could not balance himself as he pitched. This caused him to put extra pressure on his throwing arm, ultimately ending his career. This illustrates what Paul said in 1 Corinthians 12:26, "And whether one member suffer, all the members suffer with it; or one member be honored, all the members rejoice with it."

The dependence that each member of the body has on the others enhances the importance of each member in the body of Christ. Our uniqueness as individuals in the body of

Christ is magnified because we are needed. Knowing your spiritual gifts is like having a specific job description. We each have a specific job in the body of Christ without which the body will suffer.

God has given us gifts so that we can be a people of excellence. The Holy Spirit is at work to bring many to faith in Christ. Since God has loaded down our camels as a church, it is imperative that we know our spiritual gifts and how to use them. We need to develop and use them to bring home a bride for the Lord Jesus Christ.

In his book *Power Evangelism*, John Wimber has noted how the gifts of the Holy Spirit accelerate the faith of unbelievers as they are witnessed to. He says that power evangelism cuts through much resistance (arguments) that comes from ignorance or negative attitudes towards Christianity. By penetrating the inner heart and consciousness, God overcomes resistance with the supernatural, resistance that through rational means would take a lifetime or more to overcome.[1]

Before we can function in our gifting, we must know what the gifts are and what our own gift assortment is (1 Cor. 12:11).

What is a spiritual gift? C. Peter Wagner says, "It is a supernatural attribute given by the Holy Spirit to every member of the body of

Christ." This means that a spiritual gift is not a role. We have various roles as Christians. We are servants, but not everyone has the gift of service. We are witnesses, but not everyone is an evangelist. Everyone gives, but not everyone has the gift of giving. Everyone is to have faith, but not everyone has the gift of faith. Our gift is not a role or a talent. We might have some natural talent, and God can use that talent, but a gift is not of the natural. It is not a fruit of the spirit. The fruits of the Spirit create character, and the gifts of the Spirit are for ministering. Therefore, we can conclude that a spiritual gift is a supernatural ability that God has given us to minister and bear witness to Jesus. We do this through the body and to the world.[2]

C. Peter Wagner has listed the prerequisites necessary for you to find your spiritual gifts:

1. You have to be a believer.
2. You must believe that spiritual gifts are for today. God will give according to your faith.
3. You must be willing to find your spiritual gift(s) and put them to work.
4. You must want the gifts because you want to serve the body of Christ and not just to parade around and look good.

Jesus Christ has given you gifts so that you can be employable. They are enjoyable, but the main reason for them is so that you will be employable—be in service to the King.

You must pray, and God will lead you in finding your gift. The Bible says:

> If ye then, being evil, know how to give good gifts unto your children: how much more shall your heavenly Father give the Holy Spirit to them that ask him? (Luke 11:13)

As He gives you the Holy Spirit, He will reveal individually those things in the Holy Spirit ministry that he has bestowed upon you. Not everyone has the same gift.

A list of the motivational gifts can be found in Romans:

> Having then gifts differing according to the grace that is given to us, whether prophecy, let us prophesy according to the proportion of faith; Or ministry, let us wait on our ministering: or he that teacheth, on teaching; Or he that exhorteth, on exhortation: he that giveth, let him do it with simplicity; he that ruleth, with diligence; he that showeth mercy, with cheerfulness. (Romans 12:6–8)

I call the motivational gifts the backbone gifts. In other words, if you are talking about a body, many of these gifts are not honored or seen. People with these gifts are usually found in the background. These gifts are, at times, more important than the more noticeable gifts which usually have to do with speech. Paul said that they are worthy of more honor (1 Cor. 12:23–24). Could you do anything without your backbone? You cannot see your backbone, but could you do anything without one? No! We know that the people who really keep the body of Christ moving and going are those people with the gifts of help, service, and mercy.

Now, let's look at the servant's attitude:

> For I say, through the grace given unto me, to every man that is among you, not to think of himself more highly than he ought to think; but to think soberly, according as God hath dealt to every man the measure of faith.
>
> (Romans 12:3)

You need to think of yourself highly, not because you are somebody, but because of who you are in Christ. However, we have to make sure not to think more highly of ourselves than we ought.

Spiritual gifts can also be evangelistic. For instance, you have the gift of service, and you know that your neighbor and his wife just had a baby. Their grass is overgrown, and they feel frustrated with all of their new responsibilities on top of caring for their four other children. They do not have time to mow grass. So, you mow it. They'll ask why you mowed their lawn, and you can tell them that it was a gift of service and introduce Jesus to them.

Or, if you have the gift of mercy, you might be found at the emergency room ministering for hours to those who need comfort. Someone you recognize from high school comes in and sees what you are doing. He may say, "I didn't know you were like this." You say, "I'm not. In and of myself, I would not spend my time doing this, but I am saved by the blood of Jesus, and God has supernaturally given me a gift of mercy." The friend asks to know more about this gift. Now, you have the opportunity to share the gift of salvation.

Jesus stated that we will be held accountable for what we've done with what we've been given.

> But he that knew not, and did commit things worthy of stripes, shall be beaten with few stripes. For unto whomsoever much is given, of him

shall be much required: and to whom
men have committed much, of him they
will ask the more.   (Luke 12:48)

If Jesus has loaded down our camels, we
are to use those gifts to His glory in order to
bring home a bride.

God equips us with the spiritual gifts that
we need to complete the mission He has called
us to. I will share five ways you can find the
gifts that the Lord has given to you to bring
home His bride.

Explore the possibilities. Study the Bible
and what it has to say about the spiritual gifts.
It is very important that you familiarize yourself with the spiritual gifts. Four passages that
cover spiritual gifts are: 1 Corinthians 12, Romans 12, Ephesians 4, and 1 Peter 4. Inquire
about what the gifts are, how they operate, and
what they look like. You might read some
books on spiritual gifts. Talk to people who
know and have developed their spiritual gifts.

Experiment with as many gifts as you can.
What spiritual gifts have you tried? Assuming
you are under sober judgment and a sane
evaluation of yourself, by faith you begin to
find areas where you can serve. What areas in
the church can you serve? Are there needs in
your local body? It is possible that the need is
in the area of your gifting. If there is a need in

the body, then there must be some gifting in the body that can meet that need.

Give each gift a fair trial. For example, maybe you have been teaching adults and are struggling with it. You may not have the gift of teaching, or you may just need to try another age group. You might teach children very well.

Do not be discouraged if you spend six months or more in an area that turns out not to be your spiritual gift. I spent six years being a pastor, and I am not a pastor. I pastored people, but it is not my gift.

It is recorded that before Thomas Edison discovered the light bulb, he tried 10,000 times to be successful. When a newspaper reporter asked him how he felt about failing 10,000 times, Edison replied, "I have not failed 10,000 times, but rather I have found successfully 10,000 ways that it did not work." Praise God that there are not 10,000 gifts.

Examine your joy level. Do you have the joy of the Lord when you are using your spiritual gift? If you do not have joy in what you are doing, then do not do it. How many of you have said that you hated your job? God is not against you enjoying yourself while you are working for Him. He wants you to "whistle while you work."

Examine your effectiveness. A strong gift in the Lord will get results. A reporter asked

Ethel Waters why Billy Graham is such a success. She responded, "God don't sponsor no flops." God has given you a gift so that you can be successful in that particular arena. You are going to see results. That is why God has given gifts to us. He is a results-oriented God. I am not saying that you have to have results like Billy Graham, but you will see some kind of results. Evaluate your effectiveness. People generally let you know if you are being effective.

Expect confirmation from the body. People are going to recognize your gift. When I was saved, I was telling everyone about Jesus. The members of the church said, "You need to go to Bible college. You need to be a preacher." I was receiving confirmation that the call of God was on my life and that there was a spiritual gift at work in my life. As you move into this area, you need to pray and ask God, "How do I fit into the body?" As you are doing this, look for results; God's gift is going to get results. You will be happy in the employment of God.

Every member of the body is important. If you were to ask Dizzy Dean before his accident what part of his body was indispensable and would incapacitate him if he were to lose it, he would probably have said his eyes or his arm, not his big toe. The point is that every gift is important and makes up the body. If one gift is not functioning, the whole body suffers. When it functions properly, the church becomes a beautiful bride and is attractive. Remember that God's strategy of evangelism is the method of attraction. God's people are attractive just like the bride is on her wedding day. When the body is functioning supernaturally, people see excellence. People are attracted to excellence, and that is where the body of Christ should be. God has loaded us with the excellent gifts of the Holy Spirit, and through them, people will see and believe.

9

Loaded to Unload

*And the servant...departed; for all the goods of
his master were in his hand;
and he arose, and went to Mesopotamia,
unto the city of Nahor.*
—Genesis 24:10

The Lord has loaded down our camels in spiritual and material resources. Here in the United States, we have teaching tapes, books, seminars, Christian TV and radio. We have one church for every one hundred people. It is nearly impossible for an individual not to hear the gospel in the United States. He must drive past the church buildings on every corner, walk past the Christian bookstore in the malls and shopping centers, and turn past the Christian broadcast on the radio or TV. An individual would have to work at not knowing or hearing about Jesus Christ. This indicates the overwhelming resources in our country which we are accountable for. The Lord has loaded down our camels. We have every spiritual and material resource needed to bring home a bride for the Lord Jesus Christ.

Rick Joyner calls this day and age the Laodicean church age. The Laodicean church had all of the spiritual gifts and financial blessings, and they were in need of nothing. However, spiritual and material resources became a curse rather than a blessing because the Laodiceans trusted in those riches and giftings and not in the Lord Himself. It made them self-confident and not Christ dependent. Jesus Christ sternly rebuked them, and he called them to repentance. Even though the Laodicean church received such a devastating verdict of its condition, the greatest promises given to any of the churches were given to the Laodicean church if she would overcome.[1]

Moses was fairly judged for his one act of disobedience and was not allowed into the promised land. God was just in his punishment because Moses, having encountered God face to face, had received a greater revelation than his followers. Therefore, he was held to a higher standard. Teachers, James said, will receive greater condemnation (James 3:1). They have a greater revelation than their pupils.

Sodom and Gomorrah had no Bible. Not all past believers had the complete chronicle revelation as we do today. No age in history has had the revelation resources and material ability to deploy the revelation of God worldwide as this era does.

Rick Joyner also calls the age that we are in the Benjamin church age. This term parallels the Laodicean church concept. Benjamin, being the last son of Jacob, was given five times the portion of any of Joseph's brothers when they ate in Egypt (Gen. 43:34). This represents the great outpouring of both spiritual and material resources on the church:

> The abundance of spiritual food in this day exceeds all that of the other church ages, and we must take advantage of this great opportunity. The knowledge, understanding, and outpouring of direct revelation from the Lord is given to us for a reason. We are going to need every bit of it to accomplish the mandate given to us in this hour.[2]

Will we cause Him great sorrow or great joy? Will we sit down with Him on His throne or be shamed and our true nakedness exposed on the day of reckoning? Trusting in riches has caused our spiritual slumber. We must be zealous in our relationship toward God and put off everything that would seek to hinder or sever that relationship.

> No man can serve two masters: for either he will hate the one, and love the other; or else he will hold to the one, and despise the other. Ye cannot serve God and mammon. (Matt. 6:24)

Jesus did not say, "It is hard to serve God and money," or "It is tricky to serve God and money," or "It is exhausting to serve God and money." He said, "You cannot serve both God and Money" (Matthew 6:24 NIV).[3]

I heard an internationally known speaker trying to justify the prosperity doctrine. He said, "If it's a sin to be rich, Abraham was the world's biggest sinner." This brother had overlooked Genesis 24:10. It states, "All the goods of his master were in his (the servant's) hand." Why? To bring home a bride. We are blessed to be a blessing.

John Calvin wrote the following about King David:

> David knew the reason why he was reigning (prospering). It was not for his personal profit but for the common salvation of all. It is not enough to recognize the blessings of God, but we must always use them properly ....[4]

We are not to have riches to build our own kingdom. We have been blessed so that we bless the nations. We take salvation to them to bring home God's beloved.

In the past, there has always been a *resource to challenge ratio* that has stymied God's people. Ten out of the twelve spies looked at their resources against the giant Amalakites and gave a bad report, "The land is good, but it cannot be taken. We are too small."

The disciples told Jesus to send home the multitude. They felt that there were not enough resources to feed them. Jesus responded, "You feed them." "What with? We have only two loaves of bread and five fish," they said. As they obeyed the Lord and fed the multitude, the loaves and fishes increased. If we are committed to feeding the multitudes, Jesus will supernaturally multiply our resources. Jesus did not say to create the supply. He said, "Feed them." God will supply.

A widow's husband had left her in debt. She desperately appealed to Elisha to help her. "What do you have?" he asked. She replied, "A pot of oil." She was to gather as many jars as she could and to pour out her oil into them. She did as the prophet said, and the oil did not run out until the last jar was filled. If she did not have the money to pay, her two sons would have been enslaved. She sold her oil and received enough income to pay off the bondsmen. In addition, she had money with which to live.

The widow was desperate to save her two sons. If we would only be as desperate to save those who Satan seeks to eternally enslave, God would miraculously supply. He would pour out the oil —the Holy Spirit—and whatever financial resources necessary until every person, whom the Bible calls jars of clay or earthen vessels, is filled.

The principle is to unload whatever God has loaded you with, and He will continue to load you. What did the servant do with his goods? He used what he needed for the trip, and he bestowed the other goods on Rebekah and her family. Just as the servant used his goods as acts of kindness to bring home the bride, so first century Christians used "acts of kindness and charity" to penetrate the Roman world with the gospel.[5]

As a testimony of God's faithfulness, my family and I experienced this kingdom principle. At one time, I had a morning paper route to supplement our income. One morning, a truck broadsided me, and my Olds Delta 88 was totaled. The insurance company offered me $1500, and they let me keep the car. This was a blessing since before the accident the car would not sell for $500.

Soon after, we heard of some missionaries in Haiti who were in need. My wife said, "Let's give them some of the money." With the exception of our tithe portion, we ended up giving all of it to them. Beyond this, I planned to bless a Houston street preacher with the engine from the Oldsmobile. Rather than pulling the engine, he worked on the vehicle. He replaced the hood and the fender. He also made other repairs, and to my surprise, he was able to drive it to Houston.

To God's glory, the cycle continued. A Chinese congregation in our community had an old school bus that they had been trying to sell for $1500. Through one of our members, they learned of our need for a bus to pick up children in the projects. They gave us the bus. We found that the insurance and maintenance would be too expensive for us to operate it, so we gave it to another needy ministry. Several months later, a local church gave us an old white van saying, "If you can get it to run, it's yours." After a few minor repairs, it was running, and it's still running to this day. As a result of this, two missionaries from Mexico gave us vehicles. The one missionary outgrew his short-wheel based van with his eighth child. The other was going to Spain, and he gave us his truck, which I sold for $1200, to help us get to Nigeria in 1991. Our initial giving began a cycle of blessings that would not otherwise have happened.

Has God poured out enough financial resources to send individuals to be a demonstration of the gospel among the 2.4 billion lost? The biblical illustrations of the feeding of the multitude and the indebted widow resulted in God providing abundantly more than what they needed. Is God still doing that today? Yes.

In fact, according to David Barrett, as of 1988, the combined annual personal income of church members around the world, both Catholic and Protestant, amounted to a staggering 8.2 trillion dollars. Yes, God has supplied. The question is, "How are we using it?" Less than two percent was given to operate organized, global Christianity. Only one percent is spent on direct ministry outside of the Christianized world, and one-tenth of one percent is spent on the hard core unevangelized.[6]

As of 1979 in the U.S., religious property alone amounted to $130 billion. It is probably over $200 billion today. Though buildings can be necessary, the building of expensive and elaborate edifices often lacks wisdom in the light of finances needed to send out snatchers of the 2.4 billion souls plunging to hell. The gross financial output for buildings often says that we are more concerned about comfort and convenience than the destruction of souls for whom Christ died. Financing buildings was not necessary to evangelize in the first century; God provided existing structures. This was the case in Ephesus where the Apostle Paul used the school of Tyrannus to evangelize not only Ephesus but the whole province of Asia (Acts 19:9).

If acquiring a new structure is necessary then the faith we apply to seeing it built can also be applied to raising the financing of local and foreign missionaries. By doing so, the congregation gets the message that the purpose of the building is for the purpose of unloading laborers, who are equipped and financed, to reap the harvest.

Such is the case of Valley View Christian Church in Dallas, Texas.

> Last year was another pivotal year, and Valley View desperately needed a new building. Attendance now runs above 1,200, and they are bulging at the seams. In addition to normal staffing and program expenses last year, they decided to buy a plot of land at the cost of more than 1.2 million dollars.... Once again, they prayed and discussed whether or not they should raise the spending for missions another percentage point.

After much prayer and consideration, outreach was placed above their own needs. They raised missions to 39 percent of their annual budget—meaning that they now give $500,000 to the cause of Christ worldwide. Interestingly enough, on this very same Sunday morning during their Missions Fair, they were also able to make a very important announcement. The entire $1,250,000 had been paid off, and the land now belonged totally to Valley View. To me, this is an excellent illustration of the way that God blesses those churches who reach outside themselves and help others.[7]

I believe that churches like Valley View should be the norm rather than the exception. It would be if we captured God's heart for people.

Wayne Meyers, a long-time missionary in Mexico, preached that we are to turn the corruptible into the incorruptible, the perishable into the imperishable. He suggested to the students, faculty, and friends of Christ for the Nations Bible College in Dallas, Texas that they tape a sign that read "Perishable" on everything they owned. The individual possessions are then made available to God so that He might inform His people about how they are to use them. George Otis, Jr. also comments on the subject of stewardship, "Until we begin living our lives as if one hundred percent of everything we have belongs to God, we have not mastered the concept."[8]

After studying the book *Rich Christians in the Age of Hunger*, our congregation of thirty members decided to have a garage sale with the slogan, "To live more simply that others may simply live." We took things we did and did not need—furnishings, the first and/or second TVs, and items from our attics or garages. You know, those things you think you will need one day but never do. In a one-day garage sale, we raised over $1,000 for missions. We did this biannually for several years, eventually doing it to send my family to Nigeria. I wonder how many evangelists, missionaries, and other Christian workers could be supported just by believers in the United States emptying their attics, garages, and overcrowded rooms.

"The average Christian family income in 1990 was $19,280." The weekly foreign missions giving per church member was a paltry ten cents.[9] That is not exactly unloading with what we have been loaded.

As we unload, we are kept in that blessed place of sweet dependence upon God to load us again. Failing to unload can lead to curses. The prophet Malachi rebukes Israel's priests because they offered the blemished sacrifices when they had unblemished male sacrifices to offer:

> But cursed be the deceiver, which hath in his flock a male, and voweth, and sacrificeth unto the Lord a corrupt thing: for I am a great King, saith the LORD of hosts, and my name is dreadful among the heathen. And now, O ye priests, this commandment is for you. If ye will not hear, and if ye will not lay it to heart, to give glory unto my name, saith the LORD of hosts, I will even send a curse upon you, and I will curse your blessings: yea, I have cursed them already, because ye do not lay it to heart.   (Malachi 1:14–2:2)

The priests' deception of offering the blemished sacrifices rather than the good ones spoke of their relationship with God. It was a cheap one. We were not redeemed with silver or gold but by the precious blood of our Savior, Jesus Christ. When we offer less than our best, we cheapen the cost of the cross.

The priests in Malachi 2:2 were already cursed, but they did not realize it. The Laodiceans thought of themselves as most blessed, yet they were poor, wretched, blind, and naked. They failed to recognize the reality of their condition. The deceitfulness of riches had done its job of choking out the spiritual life from these two groups. The greedy person, as an idolater, has no inheritance in the kingdom of Christ and of God (Eph. 5:5). God intended the priests and Laodiceans to be blessed in order to be a blessing for all peoples. The blessing became a curse through disobedience.

Remember, we are loaded to unload. As we unload, He will load us until every member of His bride is brought safely home. He will load us down with what is needed until every pilgrim of the multitude has tasted of the Bread of Life, until every earthen vessel that can be filled is filled.

10.

Loaded with the Law

And the servant took ten camels of the camels
of his master.
—Genesis 24:10

O h, God, give me something that will
make them mad or glad. Lord, at this
point, a bad reaction would be better
than no reaction at all. I need something that
will touch their lives, that will cause them to
hear."

This is what I prayed one afternoon on
my kitchen floor. After preaching in the
streets of the projects in Bryan, Texas, and
getting no response, I had my Bible open to
Romans 3, and there I found God's answer,
specifically in verse 20, "Therefore by the
deeds of the law there shall no flesh be justified in his sight: for by the law is the knowledge of sin." A light went off in my head. I
began preaching, "If you do not accept Jesus

Christ as your Lord and Savior, then you have only one other chance to go to heaven. If you've kept God's standard without fail, you can enter God's heaven. The law by which you will be judged, if you reject Christ, is God's law—the Ten Commandments. As I share them with you, be honest. Ask yourself if you have kept each one perfectly from birth until now. Number one says..."

This was now my preaching. I got reactions. I even made up a door-to-door survey based on the Ten Commandments. At the time, Russia was becoming more open, and I heard on CBN that they were now putting the Ten Commandments in public places like schools.

We thought it would be a good survey to find out how many Americans believe the Ten Commandments are a code of conduct by which we should live and whether or not they personally keep them. I opened the survey by saying, "Communist Russia is a self-proclaimed atheistic country, and yet today, they are putting the Ten Commandments in public places to say that they believe this is a code of conduct by which to live. America is supposedly a God-fearing country. Our money says, 'In God We Trust.' Yet, the Ten Commandments are not allowed to be displayed on the walls of our public institutions." I would then add, "Do you mind if I ask you ten quick questions?" I would proceed to give them the commands while asking if they had kept each one.

Frankly, I got a good bit of flack from my Christian friends for using such tactics. "This is the age of grace and using the Law seems to lack love. Besides, you do not see anyone else evangelizing that way."

It was true. I did not know anyone doing it, and I was getting most discouraged. However, in early 1990, I met Ray Comfort at the Houston Evangelism Conference, and he encouraged me greatly. Ray was not as nationally known as he is today. Primarily using the Law, Ray preached daily in the streets of New Zealand. He had done great biblical and historical research on the use of it. God also gave him revelation and insights which I needed to hear. You can find those gems in his book, *Hell's Best Kept Secret*.

Abraham used ten camels to load down his servant. As I have mentioned, number ten represents completeness or fullness. The Ten Commandments are a complete, concise summary of the moral nature of God. We have the full revelation of how we are to conduct ourselves. By following it, we become like God.

The first four commands deal directly with our relationship with God. The last six deal directly with our fellow man, but indirectly, it reveals our relationship with God.

As John wrote:

> If a man say, I love God, and hateth his
> brother, he is a liar: for he that loveth
> not his brother whom he hath seen,
> how can he love God whom he hath not
> seen?   (1 John 4:20)

This perfect revelation of God reveals how imperfect we are in our relationship with Him. God has given us the Law to show us how far we are from Him. God's intent is for us to call on His Son for reconciliation with God the Father after we have been exposed through the Law as sinners and thus separated from Him.

God has given us the Ten Commandments to be used as a means of evangelizing the lost. Galatians 3:24 says, "Wherefore the law was our schoolmaster to bring us unto Christ, that we might be justified by faith." First Timothy 1:8–9 says,

> But we know that the law is good, if a
> man use it lawfully; Knowing this, that
> the law is not made for a righteous
> man, but for the lawless and disobedi-
> ent, for the ungodly and for sinners, for
> unholy and profane, for murderers of
> fathers and murderers of mothers, for
> manslayers.

Putting these two passages together, you come up with the fact that the Law is like a schoolmaster bringing the sinner, the ungodly, unholy individual to Christ. As believers, our purpose for using the Law is to expose the unsaved to the fact that their sin is exceedingly sinful (Rom. 7:13). We also want to relate to them the fact that they need the forgiveness of the Savior.

Romans 2:15 (AMP) says,

> They show that the essential requirements of the Law are written in their hearts and are operating there, with which their consciences (sense of right and wrong) also bear witness.

The law is written into every one of our hearts. Therefore, when we hear the Commandments, we instinctively know that they are true. Again, it is instinctive, but the Law reveals the nature or character of God, and the Bible says in Genesis 1:27 that we were originally made in His likeness. Intrinsically, we know these things to be true. The word conscience in Latin means with (con) knowledge (science). The sinner is "with the knowledge" that these are true and that he has violated the truth. As Romans 3:20 says, "Therefore by the deeds of the law there shall no flesh be justified in his sight: for by the law is the knowledge of sin." Once people come to the knowledge of sin, they see their need for a Savior.

A. B. Earle, a Baptist preacher who saw 150,000 souls come to Christ, said that he has found by long experience that the severest threatening of the Law of God has a prominent place in leading men to Christ. He says that people must see themselves as lost before they will cry for mercy and that they will not escape danger until they see it.[1]

John Wesley agreed that sin, law, and judgment should be preached before love, mercy, and grace.[2] C. H. Spurgeon said, "They must be slain by the Law, before they can be made alive by the gospel."

Usually, after I have started a casual conversation with someone I have just met, I will ask them a few diagnostic questions. These are taken from Dr. James Kennedy's Evangelism Explosion program. They will help you to identify what the individual is trusting in for his salvation. The questions are:

1. If you died tonight, do you know for certain that you would go to heaven?
2. If you did die tonight and had to stand before God, what would you say if He were to ask you why He should let you in?[3]

Most frequently, people will say that being good and obeying the Ten Commandments will get them to heaven. I usually will ask them to recite the Ten Commandments. They can sometimes quote a few but usually not all of them. I offer to go through them with the person, and I follow each explanation by asking them whether or not they have kept that particular commandment.

The Bible says that if you have broken the law in one place, you have broken it all (James 2:10). As I witness to an individual by going through the Ten Commandments, I ask them how many they have broken. I have never had anyone say that they have broken less than five.

We all have to stand before God. I tell them that they cannot justify themselves. They will not be able to go before the Judge and say, "I think you should let me in because I broke only five, and the next guy broke eight." Or, "Judge, I'd like you to consider all the people that I didn't lie to, steal from, or lust after." No, we will be judged for what we have done.

Any good deeds that you think you have done do not eliminate the fact that you have done wrong. Jesus said,

> He that believeth on Him is not condemned: but he that believeth not is

condemned already, because he hath not believed in the name of the only begotten Son of God.   (John 3:18)

A man on death row does not have to commit any more bad deeds to die. What he has done already constitutes enough to condemn him. In the same way, the law has shown that we are already condemned. We have committed enough sin. We do not have to lie, commit more thefts, or have impure thoughts. We have already done enough to send ourselves to hell.

Then, I ask the person to whom I am speaking, "Do you believe Jesus Christ lived and died a cruel death on the cross?" He died as a criminal outside the city of Jerusalem between two thieves. The Bible says Jesus was without sin. He was totally innocent, yet he was unfairly crucified for our sins.

Jesus was not the outlaw. We were. He was not the criminal. We were. He literally took our place. He died a criminal's death, and he paid the penalty for our sins. Every wrong, lustful thought, every theft, whatever it was regardless of how many times you did it, Jesus paid for it at the cross.

When Jesus was on the cross, He said, "It is finished." He was saying, "Paid in full." Jesus paid fully for your sins, so you do not have to pay for them with eternity in hell. They are finished in God's sight. Whatever the crimes committed against God, He loves you and forgives you through his Son, Jesus Christ. I would then continue by leading them to repent of their sins, receive His forgiveness, put faith in the death and resurrection, and confess Jesus as Lord.

Even as you go through those commands, you can sense the condemnation and the hopelessness. For the sinner, this is good because it surpasses the many other things that give them false security and deter them from realizing their lost state. Once they know that they are helpless, hopeless, and condemned before God's law, we can then give them God's mercy and love, if they cry out for it.

Americans have heard that Jesus loves them so much that they often do not appreciate it because they have become numb to so many words without concrete proof of their reality. "Why did He die on a tree?" "I didn't ask him to do that." "I'm glad that He is not my son." These are just a few of the comments that I have heard.

First Corinthians 1:18 says, "For the preaching of the cross is to them that perish foolishness; but unto us which are saved it is the power of God." The fact that God loved us so much that He died on a tree for us does not make sense unless we can see God mercifully taking our place for the punishment that we justly deserve.

At first, the approach of going through the Law does not appear loving, but in actuality, it is the most loving. It brings the sinner to true contrition and salvation. They will have a thorough understanding of what they have been saved from and saved to. They will know that they have sinned much and therefore been forgiven much, and consequently, they themselves will love both God and others much.

This works everywhere. I teach this in Africa. In an Anglican church, old ladies and men with religion but without a relationship to Christ have come running forward, falling on their knees, and weeping in repentance as they finally grasp the message.

Among the unreached Ijaw tribe in Nigeria, thirty men came forward after the law was shared. Most of these men have genuine fruits of salvation. "The law of the LORD is perfect, converting the soul: the testimony of the LORD is sure, making wise the simple" (Ps. 19:7). Use the perfect weapons to bring home the bride—the Law of God and then the love of God.

In his *Words of Comfort: Syllabus on Radical Evangelism*, Ray Comfort has said:

With the sickle of God's Law in your hands, you become a laborer and not a layabout, a soul-winner and not a pew warmer, an asset and not a liability.[4]

We can be loaded down and not know where to go. Being loaded is essential, but being led is equally necessary. Prayer leads the way.

11

Praying for Appointments

And he said, O LORD God of my master Abraham, I pray thee, send me good speed this day, and show kindness unto my master Abraham.
—Genesis 24:12

Our Lord is faithful to keep His covenant. God made a covenant with Abraham and obligated Himself to bless Abraham, make his name great, and make him the father of many nations (Gen. 12:2). Deuteronomy 7:9 states,

> Know therefore that the LORD thy God, he is God, the faithful God, which keepeth covenant and mercy with them that love him and keep his commandments to a thousand generations.

127

Numbers 23:19 adds,

God is not a man, that he should lie;
neither the son of man, that he should
repent: hath he said, and shall he not
do it? or hath he spoken, and shall he
not make it good?

Abraham had faith that God would do as
He promised. The servant knew of God's
covenant with Abraham. He witnessed Abraham's faith in God. Now, the servant himself
had to put his faith into that covenant to get
the bride for Isaac. When he questioned Abraham about the likelihood of success on this
mission, Abraham assured him that Yaweh,
the God who keeps His promises, would send
an angel before him, and a successful venture
in bringing home a bride was guaranteed
(Gen. 24:7).

God has promised that we also will be
successful in bringing home a bride for Jesus
Christ. He promised that His bride will be
made up of every kindred, tongue, people, and
nation (Rev. 5:9). He promised that His name
would be great among the heathen (Mal. 1:11)
and that we would have the nations as our inheritance (Ps. 2:8). Nations will come to know
and praise Jesus Christ as Lord. (See
Zechariah 8:22 and Psalm 86:9, *et al.*)

As Christ's kingdom continues to be established on every shore and among every people, God continues to demonstrate His faithfulness to Abraham and to us. He told Abraham, "And I will bless them that bless thee, and curse him that curseth thee: and in thee shall all families of the earth be blessed" (Gen. 12:3). God has been faithful to His promises, and you and I as believers in Christ are the fulfillment of the covenant to Abraham.

Yet, we are observing an Islamic world that is growing by 26,000 members every day, a resurgence in occultism and witchcraft through the New Age Movement, the cry of liberal America getting louder, and a dark cloud of violence and sex covering our streets. These evil obstacles appear too formidable for the church to penetrate. However, according to *our* power, they are not. In 2 Chronicles 20, Jehosaphat was surrounded by three armies from enemy countries. He was overwhelmed. Turning to God, he desperately prayed God's promise:

> And said, O LORD God of our fathers, art not thou God in heaven? and rulest not thou over all the kingdoms of the heathen? and in thine hand is there not power and might, so that none is able to withstand thee? (2 Chron. 20:6)

Jehosaphat called upon the covenant-keeping, sovereign Lord of the nations when other nations were seeking to subdue Judah. In prayer, Jehosaphat claimed the promises that God made to Solomon at the dedication of the temple (1 Kings 8:33–39). The promises attested that when an enemy sought to besiege the cities, anyone who would go to the temple and pray would be heard by God. This is exactly what Jehosaphat did. He declared that the enemy was greater and then claimed the covenant promise. God kept His covenant and defeated the enemy without one blow of the sword. His word will not return void. In spite of what we see, we must pray, and God will keep his word to subdue all nations. Praying the promises of our covenant says to God, "Our enemies are greater than us, but our eyes are upon you."

Please note that the promise is not the same as the possession of the promise. The promise must be acted upon before it becomes a possession. God promised that after seventy years Israel would return to Jerusalem from exile. However, if it were not for Daniel praying in the promise God made through Jeremiah, the Jews may not ever have possessed Jerusalem again. Daniel prayed in the promise until it was possessed. We must do the same. We must pray, "Thy kingdom come," until it comes in totality. We must pray that God will keep His covenant and bring forth His bride from every nation.

As we are praying, we pray to God who does not slumber. In fact, the Son of God, who established the everlasting covenant with His blood, lives to make intercession for us (Heb. 7:25). I would imagine that He is praying for us to use the spiritual authority that He has given us through prayer. This way, we will take authority over Satan and his kingdom of darkness, making the enemy His footstool (Heb. 10:13). The Lord of the harvest desires that we will pray to Him asking that He dispatch empowered laborers to harvest souls (Matt. 9:38).

We are not alone in our prayers. Though it is not reported in this account, I cannot imagine that Abraham and Isaac were not praying. Eliezer, Abraham's servant, knew of God's covenant with Abraham. The servant prays to the God of his master Abraham to give him success (Genesis 24:12). The servant appeals to God on the basis of the covenant that God made with Abraham, "And he said, 'O LORD God of my master Abraham, I pray thee, send me good speed this day, and show kindness unto my master Abraham.'"

We too should petition Father God to grant us success as we seek to lead others to

Christ. The covenant of Abraham is still in effect as there is a greater covenant through the blood of Jesus Christ. We appeal to God based on His will through Jesus Christ. Jesus said that if we ask anything according to His will, through His name, it will be done. We know that the will of God is in the very Word of God. The Scriptures to which we have previously eluded and others are the basis of our appeal to God. For instance, just as God promised Abraham that He would send an angel before his servant so that he might be successful, we also have the promise of angelic intervention to help us bring home a bride.

Angels are ministering agents to the heirs of salvation (Heb. 1:14). According to Psalms 103:20, the angels are to obey the Word of the Lord. We can appeal to God to send the angels before us to prepare those who would be heirs of salvation. The God who wishes none to perish will certainly send His angels.

In Genesis 24:13–14, the servant petitioned,

> Behold, I stand here by the well of water; and the daughters of the men of the city come out to draw water: And let it come to pass, that the damsel to whom I shall say, Let down thy pitcher, I pray thee, that I may drink; and she

shall say, Drink, and I will give thy camels drink also: let the same be she that thou hast appointed for thy servant Isaac; and thereby shall I know that thou hast showed kindness unto my master.

The servant prayed for a divine appointment. Based on the desire of God, who promised to build His church, we also should pray for God to supernaturally guide people into our path daily.

Not only did the servant pray for a divine appointment, but he also expected God to immediately answer such a prayer:

> And it came to pass, before he had done speaking, that, behold, Rebekah came out, who was born to Bethuel, son of Milcah, the wife of Nahor, Abraham's brother, with her pitcher upon her shoulder. And the servant ran to meet her, and said, Let me, I pray thee, drink a little water of thy pitcher.
>
> (Gen. 24:15–17)

Our lives and world would change if we would fervently pray for and expect divine appointments. God desires to give us divine appointments daily. Christ died in order to give life to the bride. He lives to intercede for the salvation of mankind. Angels were created for the purpose of ministering ot lost souls. All of history is based on the redemption of the human race. Therefore, we can confidently and expectantly look for God to orchestrate rendezvous with transgressors.

Steve Taylor, a Youth for Christ leader, brought together most of the local youth pastors and challenged them to plant a "praying church" on each one of the thirty-six high school campuses in Santa Clara County, California. By the beginning of 1994, they had succeeded, and today, more than a thousand high school students have joined one of the thirty-six "congregations" which make up the Church on Campus.

The students are now being trained by Taylor and his associates to pray three specific prayers before school and during class breaks. The first prayer is for themselves. The second prayer is for at least three fellow Christians on campus and the last prayer is for ten unsaved students and three teachers. This equals more than 20,000 daily prayers being lifted up on the high school campuses of Santa Clara County.[1] Not only will students and teachers be saved, but thousands of young teenagers are having a fresh, vital experience with God daily as they pray expectantly.

A divine appointment prayer asks God to send ministering angels before you to prepare those who will cross your path that day. It asks the Holy Spirit to keep you sensitive to his prompting. Thus, you will be aware of needs around you and able to share with those who have ears to hear. Such prayers believe that God is ready to routinely introduce us to those who need His healing, delivering, and saving touch.

The New Testament church believed that the covenant promises were to be fulfilled through them. The blood covenant made by Jesus Christ gave them the spiritual authority to pray for divine appointments and to see them fulfilled. John Robb points out that intercessory prayer is mentioned more than thirty times just in the book of Acts, and virtually all major breakthroughs in the outward expansion of the early Christian movement were preceded by this type of prayer.[2]

What we need is that old-time religion that prays for divine appointments and expects the Savior to deliver them.

Leonard Ravenhill aptly stated,

> The church has many organizers, but few agonizers; many who pay, but few who pray; many resters, but few wrestlers; many who are enterprising,

but few who are interceding. People who are not praying are playing.

Two prerequisites of dynamic Christian living are vision and passion, and both of these are generated in the prayer closet. The ministry of preaching is open to a few. The ministry of praying is open to every child of God.

Do not mistake action for unction, commotion for creation, and rattles for revivals.

The secret of praying is praying in secret. A worldly Christian will stop praying, and a praying Christian will stop worldliness. When we pray, God listens to our heartbeat. Hannah's lips moved, but her voice was not heard (1 Sam. 1:13). When we pray in the Spirit, there are groanings which cannot be uttered (Rom 8:26).

Tithes may build a church, but tears will give it life. That is the difference between the modern church and the early church. Our emphasis is on paying, but theirs was on praying. When we have paid, the place is taken. When they prayed, the place was shaken (Acts 4:31).

In the matter of effective praying, never have so many left so much to so few. Brethren, let us pray.[3]

Church, be encouraged! In his book, *Last of the Giants*, George Otis, Jr. reports that millions of believers are obeying the stinging words of Leonard Ravenhill:

> Happily, more Christians are praying today than ever before. (This is undoubtedly one of the primary reasons for the stunning success of global evangelization over the past several decades.) As of 1990, an estimated 170 million persons across the planet were praying daily for world mission(s). Twenty million of these were involved in full-time prayer ministry, many as members of 22 active global intercessory prayer networks or one of ten million weekly prayer groups.[4]

Much of this renewed prayer emphasis is owed to the Holy Spirit using prayer mobilizers. To learn more about the movement of prayer assemblies, I suggest that you read *That None Should Parish: How to Reach Your Community through Prayer* by Ed Silvoso. One of the collaborations that I am familiar with is that of Dr. Terry Tekyl and Renewal Ministry. They are mobilizing Methodist congregations to make room to pray. Dr. Tekyl instructs the Methodist church and others on how to organize and utilize twenty-four hour prayer rooms at their buildings.

The Moseses, Aarons, and Hurs are on the mountain praying with uplifted hands. It is time to release the Joshua Company to fight. As in the Gulf War, the air assault has led the way. Now, the ground attack will claim the final victory.

The Holy Spirit is once again bringing forth earthquaking prayers through His saints. Therefore, be ready for God to answer with divine appointments.

12

Divine Appointments

*And it came to pass, before he had done
speaking, that, behold, Rebekah came out....*

*I being in the way, the Lord led me to the
house of my master's brethren.*
— *Genesis 24:15, 27*

ndrew Merry testifies of a divine appointment in his life. Born into a
Christian family in Australia, he was a
part of a growing, family Baptist church. Even
though he had made a commitment to the
Lord at the age of 13, he became rebellious in
his teenage years, and up until the age of 28, a
large part of his life was consumed by sports,
parties and alcohol.

He decided to take a year off from being a
school teacher to travel around the world, and
he chose to visit the United States. His story
follows:

My mother was weeping over my departure saying, "Someone is watching over you." But, who is He? And, how will I get to know Him? My adventure to salvation began at the same time as my trip around the world.

It didn't take long for God to catch my attention again. He did it through an attractive young lady who sat behind me on the plane from Hawaii to San Francisco. We got on well, and I later visited her for a week in San Diego.

She was a brand new Christian, and as I was very forward with women, by the end of the week she was happy to see me leave. But,....she had been used by God to further challenge me.... I left an address and phone number for her to contact me in England, so I could return her the hospitality she had shown me in California.

I began hitchhiking throughout the USA and Canada. God continued to use Christians, ministers, and even films to keep me searching for His reality. Just outside Houston, I stood on the side of the road holding a sign saying: Australian, and a car pulled over...up the road. It reversed back, and I saw an Asian-looking guy driving.

We got on quite well as I was a Physical Education teacher, and he worked in the fitness industry and at the time was running an aerobics gym in Houston. His name was Doug Stringer.

Doug offered to put me up for the night which was not unusual in America which is full of very friendly people. He took me to his aerobic studio, and I thought that I had walked into a group of moonies; people hugged each other and called each brother and sister. I was relieved to find out that they were Christians and that the aerobics studio doubled as a ministry called Turning Point Ministries.

In Doug and the people at Turning Point, I saw the reality of the love of Jesus Christ; they cared for the people no one else cared for, they gave time, money, and efforts for people who never intended returning anything.

What I saw lined up with their message. Jesus changed their lives, and He was the reason they could and would love unconditionally. This was what I had been searching for.

At one of the meetings at the Turning Point aerobic studio in Houston in April, 1983, I asked God to forgive me for my rebellion, and I made Jesus Lord of my life.

After being discipled by Doug, I left Houston and traveled to England via Washington, Boston, and New York. In England, I got a phone call from Lynette, the Christian girl I last saw in San Diego. She nearly died of shock when I told her I had been born again, but she was delighted. We hitchhiked around Scotland together and became close friends. We eventually parted for a time, meeting again in Italy when we realized our relationship had deepened.

About 18 months after we first met on the plane in Hawaii, Lynette and I were married in Australia. Eleven wonderful years and three beautiful children later, we have a marriage which is the backbone of our ministry.[1]

Lynette, Doug Stringer, and the countless Christians Andrew Merry met on his search were all divine appointments. They were all appointed by God to point Andrew towards Jesus Christ, his Savior. There are Andrew Merrys in our life daily. Often, we may not readily recognize them because we have not seen the final result of our witness. Yet, all the points of contact played a significant role in Andrew's continued search for unconditional love in Jesus Christ.

The servant Eliezer prayed for a particular circumstance to prevail as confirmation of who Isaac's bride was to be. Behind this prayer was a confidence that God had prepared or appointed someone to be that bride.

From our reading of God's Word, we come to a conclusion that God divinely arranges meetings and circumstances. He appoints people to positions (Moses, Samuel, Jonah, Joseph, Daniel) for the salvation of His people. Jesus Christ came in the fullness of time (Gal. 4:4). Note the divine appointments that Jesus had with the woman at the well, Zachias, Bartimaeus, and others. Peter and John had a divine appointment with the lame man at the gate. Paul had a divine appointment with certain disciples at Ephesus (Acts 19).

God has appointed times and seasons for deliverance and salvation. In fact, one reason for Jerusalem's destruction was because they "did not recognize the time of God's coming " (Luke 19:44 NIV). The Word tells us that there are seasons or windows of opportunity for people to be saved. "The harvest is past, the summer is ended, and we are not saved." (Jer. 8:20). "Also for you, Judah, a harvest is appointed" (Hos. 6:11 NIV).

God has appointed for men to die once and then to receive the judgment (Heb. 9:27). He has appointed a judge and a judgment day (Acts 17:31). This God is one who chiefly desires to give life more abundantly. He does not desire the death of the wicked. Therefore, God is going to arrange for them to first receive life. He wishes none to perish but all to come to repentance (2 Pet. 3:9).

Therefore, God has divinely arranged His servants to be among his people for an appointed time to preach deliverance. What is important for us to know is that the God who arranged for Jonah to preach to Nineveh seeks to give *us* divine appointments to preach the salvation of Jesus Christ. John Wimber's definition of a divine appointment is as follows:

> An appointed time in which God reveals Himself to an individual or group through spiritual gifts or other supernatural phenomena. God arranges these encounters. They are meetings he had ordained to demonstrate his kingdom (Eph. 2:10). The term *supernatural phenomena* includes specific answers to prayers for divine appointments through the individual and others who have prayed and God's sovereign acts of mercy.[2]

Again, "We then, as workers together with him, beseech you also that ye receive not the grace of God in vain" (2 Corinthians 6:1) is for the church to take advantage of the period of grace. Jesus said, "Lift up your eyes, and look on the fields; for they are white already to harvest" (John 4:35). The harvest is plentiful. Pray the Lord of harvest will arrange for His servants to be in the harvest fields.

If you are walking in faith and in the will of God, you can confidently know that God has arranged for you to be in your current job, school, or neighborhood because there is a field of souls to be harvested for God's kingdom. Frankly, even if you are not in God's perfect will, God is a master-weaver, and He takes our wrong decisions and weaves them back into His plan. He will use you right where you are. I am not advocating missing God's perfect will. We all have missed it. I want those of you who may be missing it now to know that God will still arrange for you to meet with those who need our Savior.

If we are confident that we are where God wants us to be, we especially need to pray that God would bring people into our lives. The God who desires to have communion with His bride will answer that prayer positively. Pastor Ron Walborn of the Christian and Missionary Alliance gives such an example:

Whenever I go to a person's house, to a sporting event, or to other activities, I pray this prayer: "Lord, show me who you have prepared to receive the message of your kingdom in this place." One Saturday while waiting in a lift line at a ski resort in the Poconos, I prayed this prayer. Almost immediately, I heard a young man at least five people behind me in line cursing and swearing. As I listened to his abusive language, the Spirit of God spoke, instructing me to witness to the teenager.

I quickly told God how impossible this would be since there were four people between us. As I said this, all four people dropped out of line, and the young man and I boarded the chair lift together. Not wanting to argue with the Lord any longer, I began to share about having a relationship with Jesus. As I spoke, tears began to fill the teen's eyes. He said that he had been dating the daughter of a preacher for three months and that she had been sharing Jesus with him on a regular basis. As we neared the top of the mountain, he said through his tears, "I want to have a relationship with Jesus, too."[3]

Like this example, we see divine appointments happening on a daily basis. At your workplace, at the supermarket, ball-game, laundry mat, or wherever you happen to be. We need to recognize divine appointments that come through needs of people. Often, the physical, mental, or emotional needs are the surface problems to the root cause, their separation from God through sin.

God's goodness will often bring repentance. Be careful to use the encounter to share the gospel and to bring repentance based on their lost condition and the Savior's compelling sacrifice on the cross which saves us.

If divine appointments are out there on a daily basis, our daily prayer should reflect this, and we should be ready to act as God answers these prayers daily. As you pray for divine appointments, pray that God will put someone in your path who needs to see His power and love revealed to him. The Lord of the harvest will answer such a prayer. Because He will, we will need our feet shod with the preparation of the gospel of peace (Eph. 6:15).

Be ready to give an answer for the hope that you have in Christ Jesus (1 Pet. 3:15). We must be wise in how we act toward outsiders; making the most of every opportunity (Col. 4:5). He who wins souls is wise (Prov. 11:30).

Acting with the wisdom of God will win souls. As circumstances arise that constitute a witnessing situation, those who are ready will receive wisdom from God and act wisely to see the lost friend saved. God will give the wisdom liberally because those asking know that winning souls is His will.

After meeting Rebekah, the servant thanked God for his success, and then he prayed, "I, being in the way" (Gen. 24:27). This means, "I was on my way in doing God's will." This is how God leads us. We first put ourselves in the way of God. A life that is disposed to God is one that allows Jesus to orchestrate people and events, enabling us to share or demonstrate the gospel.

Just because your appointee does not respond positively does not mean that it is not a divine appointment. Jesus had a divine appointment with the rich young ruler. Jesus told him to sell his stuff and to give what he had to the poor. Yet, "he was sad at that saying, and went away grieved: for he had great possessions" (Mark 10:22).

Witnessing one night outside the Dixie Chicken bar in College Station, Texas, several Punkers approached and set out to make sport of our witnessing team. Being from Texas A&M University, they were filled with all kinds of learning and challenged us about creation by quoting carbon-14 experiments. Even though we shared many examples of why carbon-14 tests were not reliable and about the evolution theory being merely an unscientific religion, they did not listen and left scoffing us.

We pretty much felt like failures that evening. However, about a week later, one of the young men left a message on our answering machine saying, "This tract says, 'If your life needs changing call.' Well, I'm calling, and you're not there. Call me back. I need help." We were able to contact him, and he was led to Christ. The Word of God is powerful and penetrating.

In Genesis 24, after praying for a divine appointment, the servant runs to meet the first woman he sees approaching the well. He prayed for a divine appointment, and he expected God to answer that prayer. Then, **he put his feet to his faith**. Someone once said, "If you pray for rain, bring an umbrella." Many pray for God to open up doors but sit back and wait for nothing to happen. God answers prayers that are accompanied with faith.

When my wife went shopping, the Lord showed her how open doors actually open. Entering a store, she stepped on the rubber mat about two feet from the automatic sliding door, and the door opened. In the same manner, we see God open doors for us as we put feet to our prayer of faith. If you pray for God to bring divine appointments or for open doors for you to share, you have to put yourself in the way. You need to engage in conversations at work. You need to reach out to your neighbor.

My wife and I were going through an all time low in our ministry life. Financially, we made some mistakes and needed to take second jobs to support ourselves and the ministry. I picked up a job selling memberships at a local fitness center. The fleshly wear, attitudes, and music caused me to be prayed up daily as I entered my new mission field. I also prayed for divine appointments because daily someone new would walk through the door looking to get fit. Of course, most were way out of shape spiritually as well. I would take the prospective member on "the tour" during which I would ask probing questions. I was looking for the Holy Spirit to give an opening to share the gospel.

Many people were coming to find more than just physical exertion or fitness. The strenuous exercising and body conditioning was often a means to bury a recent hurt or to overcome inferiority and insecurity. In other words, they had come in with a spiritual need that only Jesus could meet, but they didn't know it.

Several times as the tour ended in my office, I was able to share the gospel and to bring people to Christ. The owners, being Christian, allowed me to immediately baptize them in the jacuzzi. The jacuzzi was glass enclosed, and those exercising were able to witness the baptisms. As we entered the wet area singing, the gym stopped and watched the baptism. Eventually, twelve people came to Christ during my employment at the gym. These appointments would not have taken place if the prayer of faith did not take on feet. They also would not have taken place if I had not been willing to be in the way.

In my most recent trip to Nigeria, I visited one of our missionaries working among the unreached Ijaw people, who live along the southern rivers of Nigeria. As I entered the central village of Ajakrama, many Nigerians met me and lead me to a home. Our missionary, Wilson Okotie, was not around, nor were any of his disciples, so I took it that he had instructed the young men to accommodate me at this particular home.

Wilson finally showed and informed me that I was in the wrong house; he had made other arrangements. However, this was not just anyone's house that we could disappoint, we were in the home of Chief Omawei. He was the most affluent chief in the area. He had personally funded the construction of the building for the cult that dominates the Ijaws.

Leaving the chief's home would have been a big mistake. We decided that God must be up to something, and I stayed with the chief that weekend. He attended every meeting that I held. He appeared to be taking in what was being said. The last day, I spent the afternoon with him, and through a translator, I was able to discuss the teachings with him. He told me that many of his children had been dying, and they did not know the cause. He had seen through the teaching that his cultic religion was in error, and he wanted to become a Christian. He thoroughly repented and confessed Christ.

Together, we began to break the curse of death over his family, and we pleaded protection through the blood of Jesus. Missionary Wilson Okotie reports that Chief Amawie is growing stronger in his faith daily. He goes with Wilson on the village outreaches, and he has given a home, a boat, and a building for training. He has also been used to come to the defense of Wilson when he was brought before the king on charges of converting the cult members and disturbing the gods of Igbesu through his all night prayer meetings. After hearing of the chief's testimony, the King welcomed Missionary Wilson to stay.

A heavenly arrangement was made the day that I entered the village of Ajakrama. I, like the servant in the biblical account, can testify that the Lord led me to the house of Chief Omawei. The Lord will lead you, but you must be in the way.

13

Where Are the People of Passion?

*And the servant ran to meet her, and said,
Let me, I pray thee, drink a little water
of thy pitcher.*
—*Genesis 24:17*

Where are the people of passion? Before you can answer that question, you need to know what we are talking about when we say *passion*. The word means "to suffer." If you have had the privilege to see a passion play, you know it is a play about the sufferings and crucifixion of Christ. His affection for mankind was so intense that He suffered on the cross for them.

It is often said that a young man is suffering with the passion for a young lady which means that the boy is so love crazed that he cannot think straight and may act irrationally.

Passion is having a fiery love for someone or something that will cause you to take selfless action even to the point of personal suffering. The manifestation of passion for our Lord Jesus will be seen in acts of compassion for the world's souls even to the point of personal discomfort.

The servant's passion for his master dictated his actions as he attempted to bring home a bride for the master's son. The servant's passion is demonstrated when he sees the damsel approaching the well. His faith takes feet, and he runs. The compassion of God runs after sinners. In the parable of the prodigal son, the father sees his son and *runs* to him.

Where are people of such passion today? The Booths had a passion for God, and this brought a compassion for souls. They ran and captured thousands for Christ.

Missionary J. Hudson Taylor was known as *God's Man In China* for winning so many Chinese to Christ. Before he ever went to China, his biography told of the passion and compassion that earned him his title:

> The unsaved at home were just as much a burden on his heart as the unsaved in China. Always and everywhere, he was a soul-winner.

One of his employer's patients had been a hard drinker, and now in middle life, he was suffering from senile gangrene. His condition was serious and his hatred of everything to do with religion so intense that it seemed hopeless to try to influence him. [1]

Hudson Taylor wrote:

The disease commenced as usual; insidiously, and the patient had little idea that he was a doomed man and probably had not long to live.

I was not the first to attend him, but when the case was transferred to me, I became very anxious about his soul. The family with whom he lived were Christians and from them I learned that he was an avowed atheist and very antagonistic to anything religious. They had, without asking his consent, invited a Scripture Reader to visit him, but in great passion, he had ordered him from the room. The vicar of the district had also called, hoping to help him, but he had spat in his face and refused to allow him to speak. His temper was described to be as very violent, and altogether, the case seemed as hopeless as could well be imagined.

Upon first commencing to attend him, I prayed much about it but for two or three days said nothing of a religious nature. By special care in dressing his diseased limb, I was able to lessen his sufferings considerably, and he soon began to manifest appreciation of my services. One day, with a trembling heart, I took advantage of his grateful acknowledgments to tell him what was the spring of my action and to speak of his solemn position and need of God's mercy through Christ. It was, evidently, only a powerful effort of self-restraint that kept his lips closed. He turned over in bed with his back to me and uttered no word.

I could not get the poor man out of my mind, and very often through each day, I pleaded with God, by His Spirit, to save him ere He took him hence ....After continuing this for some time, my heart sank. It seemed to me that I was not only doing no good but perhaps really hardening him and increasing his guilt.

One day after dressing his limb washing my hands, instead of returning to the bedside, I went to the door. ...I saw his surprise as it was the first time since opening the subject that I had attempted to leave without saying a few words for my Master.

I could bear it no longer. Bursting into tears, I crossed the room and said, "My friend, whether you will hear or whether you will forbear, I must deliver my soul." I went on to speak very earnestly, telling him how much I wished that he would let me pray with him.

To my unspeakable joy, he did not turn away, but replied, "If it will be a relief to you, do." I need scarcely say that falling upon my knees I poured out my soul to God on his behalf. Then and there, I believe, the Lord wrought a change in his soul. He was never afterwards unwilling to be spoken to and prayed with, and within a few days, he definitely accepted Christ as his Savior. The now happy sufferer lived for some time after this change, and he was never tired of bearing testimony to the grace of God....

Regarding this situation, I have often thought of the words, "He that goeth forth and weepeth, bearing precious seed, shall doubtless come again with rejoicing, bringing his sheaves with him." Perhaps if there were more of that intense distress for souls that leads to tears, we should more frequently see the results that we desire. Sometimes, while we are complaining of the hardness of the hearts of those we are seeking to benefit, the hardness of our own hearts and our own feeble apprehension of the solemn reality of eternal things may be the true cause of our want of success.[2]

The passion for God caused Hudson Taylor to run after the sinner. His empathy for souls caused him to weep over the lost state of his patient. The compassion of God that weeps over sinners breaks the stony heart.

Nehemiah and Jeremiah wept over the sins of the people and their forefathers. David wept over his enemy King Saul. Jesus wept over the city of Jerusalem which rejected and crucified Him. We will sow in tears before we reap with joy.

After much toil in trying to lead lost friends, relatives, and acquaintances into salvation with seemingly no results, we are apt to give up. God is interested in breaking our hearts before he breaks theirs. God is not merely after a soul, but He is developing the hearts of soul winners.

"I am a broken hearted man," confessed the outstanding Wesleyan preacher, John Smith:

My God has given me such a sight of the value of precious souls that I cannot live if souls are not saved. Oh, give me souls or else I die.[3]

Dick Eastman comments:

Indeed, one can never underestimate the power of brokenness before the Lord. It is unfortunate that much of our praying is devoid of deep-felt compassion. This is especially regrettable since nothing seems to hold more power in touching God than a broken spirit.[4]

The passion for God that leads to a compassion for souls will have power. As our Savior knew, bearing witness for Him could not be done without it. He tells the frightened disciples to tarry in Jerusalem and to wait for the enduement of power from on High. It takes power to develop character that will make you a credible herald of the gospel and give the message efficacy.

It takes power to overcome insecurities, inferiorities, and fears. Paul came in weakness, fear, and much trembling, but his passion for God and compassion for souls brought the power of God which overcame all his human frailties (1 Cor. 2: 1–5).

The servant, Eliezer, did not fear losing face, reputation, or image. He did not think, "What if I'm mistaken, and she's not the one. I'll appear so foolish." In fact, he seemed unaware of himself altogether as he runs without caution to the damsel.

The servant's passion was to please the father and to see Isaac have the love of his life. He was oblivious to anything else. This love for God and compassion for sinners to be wed to the Son of God will empower us to drive away all fears. The Holy Spirit will pour out power, enabling us to overcome the fears that seek to muzzle us. Since passion for God and mercy for humanity is a condition of the heart that every believer is to have, we have no excuse for our "guilty silence."

Someone said to James Farmer, former Director of the Commission on Racial Equality, "What do you want from me? I'm just an innocent bystander." Farmer answered, "If you are a bystander, you are not innocent."[5]

If we are bystanders, we are not innocent. We are guilty. We are guilty of a lack of passion for God and compassion for men. If we possessed these qualities, they would move God to send His power to untangle our feet and to loose our tongues for His glory and for His bride.

Could a mariner sit idle if he heard the
    drowning cry?
Could a doctor sit in comfort and just
    let his patients die?
Could a fireman sit idle, let men burn
    and give no hand?
Can you sit at ease in Zion with un-
    reached peoples damned?[6]

Are you a person of passion?

14

"And He Worshipped"

And the man bowed down his head,
and worshipped the Lord. And he said,
Blessed be the Lord God of my master
Abraham, who hath not left destitute my
master of his mercy and his truth:
I being in the way, the Lord led
me to the house of my master's brethren.
—Genesis 24: 26– 27

In his success, the selfless servant gives the most striking example of what the church ought to be. After each step of success, the servant bows down and worships (Gen. 24:26, 52). The most tempting times for us are not those of despair but occasions of prosperity and success. For this reason, Paul cautioned his readers, "No, I beat my body and make it my slave so that after I have preached to others, I myself will not be disqualified for the prize" (1 Cor. 9:27 NIV).

It was after David finally succeeded in becoming King that he fell into adultery with Bathsheba. Sexual promiscuity was only the surface cause of a deeper root problem that had sprung up in David's heart from his success—pride. David's sin of passion was in reality a sin of pride. Pride said, "I deserve Bathsheba, and I want her, and I will have her." His other sin of pride, found in counting his army, brought a plague that killed 70,000 (2 Sam. 24).

God's servants are still plagued with the pride that keeps count of God's victories. It is not as obvious today because we are too sophisticated. We preface our reports with, "*Give God the glory!* One-hundred-twenty-five were saved today." We are willing to give Him glory as long as the people were saved through us.

The servant truly worshipped God for his success. True worship is honoring God for who He is and what He has done. There was no sense of pride in this humble servant, and his immediate act of worship kept it from infiltrating his heart.

Soul winners must be true worshippers of God. Worshipping God defuses pride and keeps us humble. The literal meaning of the most commonly used word for worship illustrates this humble attitude. The Greek word for *worship*, προσκυνε'ω (pros-koo-neh'-o), means "to kiss towards or to prostrate oneself." The word picture is that of a peasant bringing to a feudal Lord the portion of the harvest that is owed him. They would lay their gifts before his throne. As the King stretched out his right hand with the signet ring, the peasant would kiss towards it without touching it in honor of his lordship. Anything fruitful that comes from our lives has originated in God. We lay all of our crowns graciously before Him in worship, and we declare Him as the true owner of it all.

This is true evangelism. He is the Lord of the harvest. He is the Lord of hosts who is moving His angels to destroy our enemies. He is allowing us to go in and to plunder the enemy's territory of souls held captive.

With the greatest harvest of souls taking place today, it is no coincidence that men who have a prophetic voice in our country say that the key element for leadership in the 90s is humility. In this last harvest, God will not give his glory to another (Isa. 48:11). God's power and ability is going to grace the true worshippers. The evidence of His grace will be the humble servant being rewarded with the souls of men won to Christ.

The servant's worship demonstrated a sweet, total dependence on God. Without God, how would the servant have known whom to pick as the bride? Where would the camels and the proper gifts have come from if God had not blessed his master, Abraham? We, like the servant, have nothing to offer God but our lives for His use. We are poor and without the spiritual ability to accomplish anything on our own. We can do nothing that will count in eternity apart from the life of Jesus Christ. Paul said, "But by the grace of God I am what I am" (1 Cor. 15:10). By the power and giftings of the Holy Spirit, Paul was who he was.

As witnesses for Christ, are we winsome in and of ourselves? Unless the Spirit endues us with His life and presence, no souls will be saved. Worship is saying, "God, I cannot do it without you." It is this worshipping witness that God uses. He uses those who declare themselves weak. As Paul said, "As sorrowful, yet always rejoicing; as poor, yet making many rich; as having nothing, and yet possessing all things" (2 Cor. 6:10). We have no life in and of ourselves that can produce spiritual life in others, but God gives us His life. We are given the words of life by Jesus Christ. As we speak, the Holy Spirit produces, and God gives the increase (1 Cor. 3:7).

Hannah was a true worshipper of God. If you can recall the story that begins in 1 Samuel 1, Hannah and Peninnah were the wives of Elkanah. Peninnah possibly had up to ten sons. Hannah was barren. As barrenness was looked upon as a curse from God, it was most trying for Hannah to annually go to Shiloh to worship. It must truly have been a sacrifice of praise from Hannah's lips.

You can picture her tagging along behind while Peninnah struts into the temple at Shiloh like a proud peacock with her ten sons. Elkanah, sympathetic to his wife, would always give Hannah a greater portion to sacrifice. I suggest that Elkanah represents our Lord. As we come to God, we say, "Lord, I am barren, and I have nothing to offer you, but here I am." The Lord says, "I do not love you because you produce. I love you for who you are. Here is a gift to use as a sacrifice for me." God gives us gifts and abilities to be used as a love offering to Him.

The name Hannah means "grace." Hannah probably tried endlessly to become pregnant. She might have eaten certain foods that someone suggested would make her more fertile, and she probably examined every area of her sexual relationship with Elkanah.

Finally, her barrenness brought her to brokenness (1 Sam. 1:10). Hannah became broken over any ability she thought she had to become fruitful. The brokenness led her to total dependence on God as the Lord of life to bring forth her seed (1 Sam. 1:11). She vows to dedicate the son to the Lord's service, and the Lord graces her with Samuel as promised through Eli. The name Samuel means, "Because I asked him of the Lord." This reveals Hannah's dependence on the Lord's grace to give life.

If you have been an ardent worker in the harvest fields, you have probably experienced seasons of drought and barrenness where little, if any, fruit of souls being saved can be seen. Going to church, or better yet a pastor's conference, is a sacrifice of praise because your ministry peers ask the painful qualifying question, "How many members are you running now, brother?" You have tried all of the church growth methods of the 2,000 fastest growing churches in America, but none seem to work for you. Your barrenness did or will bring you to brokenness.

You cannot produce life. Your brokenness brings your heart to surrender to the Lordship of Jesus Christ in a deeper way. You declare to God that any sons and daughters received will honor Him and give Him glory. They are His and not yours. God then graces you. His grace produces worship in you that declares your dependence on Him.

Worship gives honor to whom honor is due. If God gives life and the increase, no glory or honor should go to Apollos, Paul, or Cephas. It is honor due only to God. The servant, Eliezer, was doing just that when he "bowed down and worshipped."

The donkey which Christ rode down the Mount of Olives during what is known as the triumphal entry into Jerusalem was asked by his fellow burrows how his day fared. "Oh, it was a day like none other," he said. "A crowd met me at the top of Mount Olivet and lead a procession of singing about me. They laid down blankets and palm leaves before my path as if I were a king. Some even got so carried away as to make claims of deity. I had a great day." It seems that many of us are taking Jesus for a ride. We do ministry for God but are quick to receive the praise of men. The purpose of our lives is to glorify Him and Him alone. Those who are ready to lay down their titles and personal accolades for the testimony of Jesus will be used of God in these last days. Worship that honors God alone will help keep us there.

We are coming into the Davidic age of the church. Saul killed his thousands, but David killed his tens of thousands. The Saul era is where big ministries and big money were idolized. Man and his ministry had been lifted up. God is bringing that down. In fact, it is dead. We can be thankful for the Saul era.

Souls were saved, and the kingdom advanced at times.

Now, a new era has come. A remnant of ragtag worshippers has been trained in the school of obscurity: lowly servants who, like David, love and worship God, servants whose sole desire is to see the King, His kingdom come, and His will be done. This is the type of person God will use mightily in these last days. Our Lord has prepared an army of them. Are you in this army?

As we have already pointed out, all life comes from God. Therefore, the institutions, ministries, and preachers are not the source but only the channel of that life. The servant did not worship Abraham but the God of Abraham. "That, according as it is written, He that glorieth, let him glory in the Lord" (1 Cor. 1:31). Man is not to glory in men (1 Cor. 3:21).

I have made a modern day paraphrase of something that C. S. Lewis wrote in *Mere Christianity* to illustrate how we sometimes act. Taking the glory due God is like your son asking you for money to buy you a Christmas gift. He buys it, gives it to you, and proudly tells his friends what he gave his Dad. This is childish and often how we act. God is seeking those who know the truth; we have nothing to give to God unless the Spirit of God invests in us. If that little boy gives the gift to his dad and says, "Thank you Dad for giving me the money to buy a gift for you. I love you and hope you like what I bought." Any father's heart would leap with gladness. This is what we say in worship. "Jesus, I know You have given to me everything that I have. I thank You. I pray that You are pleased with what I have done with what You have given me."

Our worship produces faith. An element of worship is thanking God for what He has done. "As for me," prayed the servant, "the Lord has guided me in the way to the house of my master's brothers." The thanksgiving yields to a greater faith in God. It creates a trust in God for what He will do.

As we sincerely thank God for His accomplishments through our human frailty, we add to our faith in what He will do in the future. The worshipper, David, grew in his faith after killing the lion and the bear. This enabled him to tackle Goliath. On the other hand, the Israelites, in spite of awesome wonders performed by the Lord, failed to have the attitude of worship and gratitude. They grumbled and complained until D-Day came. The day that they were to enter victoriously into the promise land turned, instead, into a day of fear and shrinking back from their huge enemies. As thanksgiving feeds your faith, ingratitude feeds unbelief and doubt.

Thanksgiving gives you eyes of faith. You look not to your own abilities but to the God who cannot fail. Our faith is in God, and worshipping God in thanksgiving says, "I believe you are who you say you are. I believe you will do what you said you would do." The servant thanked the God of Abraham for being gracious and true to His promise.

Finally, our witness is worship! Another word used for worship, λατρεν'ω (lat-ryoo'-o), means "a service rendered to God." Once we have the mind of glorifying God in all we say, our witnessing becomes a lifestyle of worship to God.

As you use your spiritual gift (and all gifts can be used effectively in evangelism), you are worshipping in spirit as you proclaim the truth of the glorious gospel of our Lord, Jesus Christ. Our gifts are not confined to a building but are signs that are to accompany those who go in the name of Christ. Therefore, our worship is not something confined to a building on Sunday morning.

Our lives are to be living sacrifices through our daily witness of the one who died for us. This is our reasonable worship (Rom. 12:1). Witnessing will mean conflicts, ridicule, and humiliation. As we share His love in the midst of a hostile world, we say with our lives, "Jesus, I love you and honor you above my own reputation, my need to be liked, and my very life."

God inhabits the praises of His people. As the praises went forth in the temple, the glory of God filled it (2 Chron. 5). You are that house of worship. As you worship through witnessing, expect God to be present. He is Immanuel, "God with us," who shall save His people from their sins through you. The Spirit of the Lord shall rest upon you to set the captive free. God will be present and will glorify His Son, Jesus, through your worshipful witness.

15

Urgent: Meat Eaters Wanted

And there was set meat before him to eat:
but he said,
I will not eat, until I have told mine errand.
—Genesis 24:33

I n the Scriptures, I have found that when people are in haste sin is not too far behind. However, there is one area where God consistently has us in a place of urgency. This is an urgency to see souls saved. This urgency comes from the fact that life is short for us earthlings. Many Scriptures bear out life's brevity and therefore the importance to be saved:

And as it is appointed unto men once to die, but after this the judgment.

(Heb. 9:27)

Seek ye the LORD while he may be found, call ye upon him while he is near. (Isa. 55:6)

Thus saith the LORD, In an acceptable time have I heard thee, and in a day of salvation have I helped thee: and I will preserve thee, and give thee for a covenant of the people, to establish the earth, to cause to inherit the desolate heritages. (Isa. 49:8)

And shall lay thee even with the ground, and thy children within thee; and they shall not leave in thee one stone upon another; because thou knewest not the time of thy visitation. (Luke 19:44)

Watch therefore: for ye know not what hour your Lord doth come. (Matt. 24:42)

Notice the urgency to be active (win souls). God keeps us in this place of urgency by telling us that He is uncertain when He is coming back, but He is certain that He is returning. Therefore, we have urgency because the time grows shorter for the scriptural fulfillment of Christ's return. **We need to live each day as if it is going to be our wedding day—the day when our union with Christ**

is complete. It is the day we meet Christ in the air at the rapture or in heaven after our physical death.

Our servant had a similar sense of urgency. Time was growing short for the promise to be fulfilled in Abraham's life, for death was closing in on the aged patriarch. The combination of Abraham's ensuing death and the unfulfilled promise made the call to get a bride for Isaac a most pressing one.

The other element that gives us a sense of urgency to win the lost is the horrible reality of an eternal hell. The apostle Paul had an understanding of the judgment seat of Christ and the horrors of hell. He said that we must all appear before the judgment seat of Christ; that every one may receive the things done in his body, according to that he hath done, whether it be good or bad.

> Knowing therefore the terror of the Lord, we persuade men; but we are made manifest unto God; and I trust also are made manifest in your consciences. (2 Cor. 5:10–11)

Jesus knew it. He said that if your eye causes you to sin, it is better for you to gouge it out and go through life blind than for your whole body and soul to be cast into hell (Matt.

5:29). Jesus is not merely exaggerating to get people to take sin seriously. He is giving us the reality of a horrible hell. The hell that Jesus passed through in his trial and crucifixion, in order for us to escape hell's eternal pain, is enough to tell me to avoid it. Remember —hell is final. It has no parolees. There is no time off for good behavior. (See Luke 16, the parable of the rich man and Lazarus.) After earning the right to be heard, this is a message that still needs to be told. In a world where people do everything they can to avoid pain and suffering, a message of eternal darkness with gnashing of teeth (or major league pain) in hell may find an open ear.

A message, as equally urgent, to be delighted in is not to miss the glories of heaven where there is no more crying, sorrow, or dying. The fulfillment of a place where there are no light bills, the streets are gold, and everyone has a luxury apartment in a massive condominium built by God.

The servant's message to Laban, in order to get his consent to take Rebekah back as Isaac's bride, was,

> And the LORD hath blessed my master greatly; and he is become great: and he hath given him flocks, and herds, and silver, and gold, and menservants,

and maidservants, and camels, and
asses.   (Gen. 24:35)

This must have sounded like heaven to
Laban.

God does not wish any to perish. That is
why he built a heavenly city for us (2 Pet. 3:9;
Heb. 11:10). As previously mentioned, heaven
will be an awesome place. Yet, missing heaven
is not about missing a place but a person.
What makes it heaven is that God is there.

Jesus tells the story of the great banquet
in Luke 14. He sends his servants out to tell
those who had been invited that the food is
ready, yet they refused to come.

And the lord said unto the servant, Go
out into the highways and hedges, and
compel them to come in, that my house
may be filled.   (Luke 14:23)

Today, it would be like going to the poor
in the United States and saying that the
President is throwing a huge banquet in
Madison Square Garden:

"The people he invited did not show up,
so he told me to invite you."

"The President of the United States
wants me?"

"Yes, and it is all you can eat."

I am sure that those who have been outcast would enjoy the food, but the best would be the honor of having fellowship with the President. God invites us to His banqueting table. Jesus invites us to a love relationship as His bride. We do not want anyone to miss out.

The servant moved with overriding urgency because he needed to get the God-ordained bride and bring her to her appointed husband. Our urgency is due to the fact that the return of the bridegroom is more imminent, and the time for people to receive the promise of salvation is short.

Millions pass daily into the horrific hell intended for the devil and his angels. Even unbelievers are aware that the sun is setting on the earth's existence as evidenced by the production of books and movies predicting the world's upcoming destruction. Most of all, our passion for our Savior to have His bride and therefore, our compassion for people to become His bride is our utmost motivation. It compels us to go and share the good news.

There are many instances throughout this account where the servant portrays a sense of urgency. Looking at Genesis 24:31–33, we see that after the many miles of traveling, the tired, hungry servant is offered a refreshing meal from Laban, but the servant refuses to eat until he tells his business. Now, that is a sense of urgency. Again, the servant does not think of himself, his tired old body, or his growling stomach. His only thoughts are of his master's son needing a bride.

This is the urgency that the church of Jesus Christ in America is lacking. Our main business here is not to enjoy the finest foods and to drive the fanciest cars. Our main business is to bring home a bride for the Lord Jesus Christ.

In John 4, Jesus is ministering to the Samaritan woman at the well while the disciples were in town for lunch. The disciples came back and saw Jesus in conversation. The woman leaves their company and goes to town and says, "Come, see a man, which told me all things that ever I did: is not this the Christ" (John 4:29)? Then, they went out of the city and came unto Him. Meanwhile, the disciples were urging Him to eat, but Jesus responded,

> My meat is to do the will of him that sent me, and to finish his work. Say not ye, There are yet four months, and then cometh harvest? behold, I say unto you, Lift up your eyes, and look on the fields; for they are white already to harvest. (John 4:34–35)

I want you to see Jesus' vivid teaching. The question is about physical nourishment and satisfaction. Jesus is obviously speaking of the spiritual nourishment and satisfaction that moves Him but not His disciples at this juncture. The nourishment is to finish the redemptive work that the Father started in Noah. He clarifies this by saying that the harvest is now.

Samaritans are coming up the road just as Jesus is speaking. As He sees them coming He points to the Samaritan crowd and cries, "Behold, this is your harvest field" (John 4:35, author's paraphrase). As you can see, Jesus is teaching His disciples that His church is a missionary church. His father's redemptive work is for all peoples.

This whole incident was an indictment on the lackluster spiritual life of the disciples. The disciples, who lived with Jesus, had just returned from the town after filling their bellies. The Samaritan woman, who had only known Jesus for a few moments, goes into the very same town and brings out its people to see Jesus.

There is a harvest field all around us. Do you behold it? If we do behold it, do we have that sense of urgency to bring others to see Jesus and to drink of the living water? Do you have a stomach for Jesus' meat? Or, does the thought of proclaiming the good news of Jesus Christ give you indigestion? When was the last time you fasted for souls? When was the last time you were so involved in ministering Christ to the lost that food didn't enter your thinking because your nourishment came from doing the work of Jesus Christ.

Often times, this has been our privilege as we ministered in the streets here in the U.S. and in Nigeria, West Africa. During those times, to have eaten would have been to miss out on the real meal. The true value-meal is in being a part of God's redemptive work in Christ. What Jesus told the disciples is also a stinging rebuke to us! We do not know of the meat that Jesus has to eat.

Gluttony makes us spiritual sluggards. We are drowsy, and our spiritual eyes are made dull because of this god of the belly. The number of restaurants and the bombardment of food advertisements have made us a nation that lives to eat rather than one that eats to live. The church has followed suit.

Fast and pray to recover your spiritual sight. Fast and pray to recover that sense of urgency to see the captive set free and liberty preached to the imprisoned. Fast and pray until you become broken over what breaks God's heart. A good book on fasting is *God's Chosen Fast* by Arthur Wallis.

A prophet speaks not only the truth of God but the heart of God. This heart is one of zeal and urgency that God wishes his church to have until the work is accomplished as found in Isaiah 62:6:

> I have set watchmen upon thy walls, O Jerusalem, which shall never hold their peace day nor night: ye that make mention of the LORD, keep not silence.

Jesus wants us to pray until He makes Jerusalem a praise on the earth, until His kingdom comes and His will is done in every tribe, tongue, and nation.

Today, many Christians are quoting Revelation 22:17, "And the Spirit and the bride say, 'Come.'" In doing so, they are expressing their desire for Jesus Christ to return soon and rapture His church.

The church is to look for Christ appearing, and there will be a time the church says, "Come, Lord Jesus." However, that statement now is premature. The Spirit of God is not prompting the church with that cry at this time. The Spirit of God is always in perfect unison with the Father and the Son. God the Father and the Son are saying the same thing that Abraham and Isaac told their servant, "Go!"

Revelation 22:17 is in the last book of God's total revelation to mankind. The verse is in the last chapter of the last book of the Bible. Therefore, all revelation will have been fulfilled by Revelation 22, meaning everyone who could be saved has been saved. Then, the Spirit and the bride (the church) say, "Come." Until then, the Father and the Son have said, "Go!" **The command of the Father who says "Go!" must be completely obeyed before the Spirit and the bride can say "Come."**

The servant received the command of father Abraham and of the son Isaac to go, and there was no stopping; no stopping for food or any personal desire until he had brought home the bride. The servant had no peace until the bride was safe in the arms of the son of his master. His meat was to finish the work for which the father had sent him.

16

Why You Need a Testimony (And Not a Title)

And he said, I am Abraham's servant. And the Lord hath blessed my master greatly; and he is become great: and he hath given him flocks, and herds, and silver, and gold, and menservants, and maidservants, and camels, and asses.
—Genesis 24:34–35

The Bible gives many examples of people with titles but not true authority who are put up against those with true power but no title. Some examples include: Ahab *vs.* Elijah, Pharaoh *vs.* Moses, and Nebuchadnezzar *vs.* Daniel. Remember that the only title Eliezer held was that of servant. I would take the power and presence of God over a title any day. So did the Apostle Paul. This is why he saw his titles as nothing compared to the all surpassing greatness of knowing Christ.

Paul had many titles from his days as a Jewish scholar and as an Apostle of the Lord, Jesus Christ. Paul never used a title to impress men. Frankly, the heathen of his day would not have been impressed anyway.

The pagans of our day are also not impressed with religious titles. In fact, with the recent fall of TV evangelists and preachers, it would probably be wise not to use a title. Often, when you use a title, the common person cannot identify with your testimony. Excuses such as, "Well, you are a preacher. God will not work that way for me," will be expressed. Other reasons why you need a testimony and not a title are as follows:

1. *Those with the testimony of Jesus Christ will go to heaven, and those with only a title will not.* You can say, "I was a deacon, leader of the choir, or district overseer." But, without a relationship with God, He will say, "I never knew you: depart from me" (Matt. 7:23).

2. *Satan cannot hurt those with a testimony until their time of testifying is over.* Live boldly and confidently. God will preserve you until your testimony is over. No weapon formed against you shall prosper.

3. *You cannot overcome Satan with a title, but you do overcome with a testimony.* Satan is not afraid of who you are but of the living Christ who is in you: "Greater is he that is in you, than he that is in the world" (1 John 4:4).

4. *You cannot proclaim the gospel effectively without a testimony.* The Thessalonians believed because of the life of God in Paul.

5. *Most people cannot transfer their titles, but all can transfer their testimonies.* Psalm 71:18 says:

> Now also when I am old and grey-headed, O God, forsake me not; until I have showed thy strength unto this generation, and thy power to every one that is to come.

We can transfer testimonies to the next generation and the next-door neighbor.

The servant used his testimony to win Laban's trust. His enigma was in how to convince Laban that he should allow his sister to go to a strange land with this mysterious traveler. After getting permission to tell why he has come, Eliezar first gives Laban some personal background. He told him whose servant he was, the orders he had, and the testimony of God's leading him on the journey. He imparts all of this before asking for Rebekah's hand in marriage to Isaac.

191

The servant preempted his question with a testimony of the mighty work of God. He shared how God was with his master, Abraham. God had made him great (Gen. 24:35). Laban had to have thought: If Abraham is great, how much greater must his God be? The testimony goes on to enumerate the riches of Abraham which speaks of Yahweh as the great provider. The angel leading the way says that God is providential. Eliezer told of his specific prayer for God's leading. Then, God's immediate and specific answer proved this trip was not a scheme dreamed up in the imagination of Abraham. Rather, it was led and guided supernaturally by God. The answered prayer let Laban know that God is personal.

Relating this testimony, Eliezer demonstrated wisdom. The servant was not asking for Laban to entrust him with silver, gold, flocks, and herds. Eliezer was asking Laban for his priceless sister. Eliezer had the task of quickly winning the trust of Laban. Quite frankly, if I was going to trust my daughter with a stranger who just pulled in from California, I would need to know some specifics, but more than that, I would need to know it was God's supernatural leading.

When we approach the unbeliever with Jesus Christ, we often are also strangers looking for their hand in marriage. We have a

Master whose Son is in need of His bride. How can we communicate to the unbeliever that the person of Jesus, who is seeking their hand in marriage, can be trusted?

We tell them how good God has been to us since we have entrusted Him with our lives. In a testimony, you give your personal experience of how your life has changed through your relationship with the Almighty God. Your testimony may include a number of things: miraculous healings, restored relations, provisions, and growth. It may be of the past or present. Either one gives the unbeliever hope and faith that God will do the same for them. Your testimony is effective because it enables you to identify with your prospect. All of the events that make up your life can be used to identify with a myriad of people.

This is inferred by Abraham's giving instructions to his servant that he was not to go to the Canaanites but to Abraham's country and kinsmen (Gen. 24:3–4). There may be several reasons for this directive. One seems to be that Abraham's people were, perhaps, upright and thus more receptive to Abraham's God. Also, there would be no cultural barriers to overcome.

The principles of going to the most receptive people and to those of similar cultures

and backgrounds were employed by Jesus and
Paul as a strategy. In sending out the twelve
disciples, Christ commanded them saying:

> Go not into the way of the Gentiles,
> and into any city of the Samaritans en-
> ter ye not: But go rather to the lost
> sheep of the house of Israel.
>
> (Matthew 10:5-6)

Likewise, Paul, on his missionary tours,
made it a practice to visit the synagogues first.
Paul was a Hebrew of Hebrews. He could
readily identify with his Jewish brethren.
Also, Christ and Paul understood that God
had prepared many Jews for the gospel. Plus,
divine appointments awaited the disciples and
the Apostle Paul as they entered these cities.

Paul was always ready to use his multifac-
eted background to help save someone. He
was constantly looking for an occasion to
identify with the lost so as to introduce Christ.
(See Acts 17:18-34.) Paul asked for prayers for
opportunities to speak the mystery of Christ.
He tells us to live looking for opportunities to
share with those without the faith. In Colos-
sians 4:3-5 it says,

> Withal praying also for us, that God
> would open unto us a door of utterance,

to speak the mystery of Christ, for which I am also in bonds: That I may make it manifest, as I ought to speak. Walk in wisdom toward them that are without, redeeming the time.

God will provide opportunities for you to use your past experiences to identify with people. Believe that God will arrange such meetings to enable a natural sharing of the gospel. Listen to the unbeliever's background and current situation. It will give some indication of how God has been preparing them.

I grew up in a Catholic home, so I have something in common with approximately 900 million people. I have brought several members of the Catholic faith to a personal relationship in Jesus Christ.

The first twenty-one years of my life, I was consumed with baseball. On a recent flight, I sat next to a professional baseball pitcher who was recovering from surgery on his arm. I could relate to him because I pitched in high school and college. I even tore a tendon in my arm that took more than a year to mend. As we talked, we found that we had common acquaintances from both the pro and college ranks. All of these similarities made an easy transition into how my injuries had led me to a relationship with Christ.

Being open about *your* personal life helps the other individual to open up and share about their personal life and needs. The Holy Spirit will then give you wisdom in how to reach out and demonstrate the reality of God's love and power.

Your testimony should have three fundamental parts. It should first tell of your life before salvation in Jesus Christ. Secondly, your testimony should tell of when you put your trust in Christ's death and resurrection. Finally, your testimony should show your life now and what has happened since you trusted in Him.

I suggest having both a short and a long version of your testimony ready so that you can "be ready always to give an answer to every man that asketh you a reason of the hope that is in you" (1 Pet. 3:15). *The Evangelism Explosion Workbook* by Dr. James Kennedy offers good instruction on how to develop and use your testimony.

The testimony tells of how you were separated from God, how you met God, and how the relationship has been since. The testimony is a story of two strangers meeting, falling in love, and living happily ever after. Think of your testimony as if you are giving an interview to a snooping news reporter who wants all the details about your relationship. Give them all the details of your intimate love affair that consists of purity and total commitment to the bridegroom, Jesus Christ. Tell them how your lover has showered you with His goodness. Your testimony is about your relationship with the person, Jesus Christ.

People will not put their trust in an abstract title. If they do, it is idolatry. We want them to put their trust in the greatest person who ever walked the earth. He has the title King of Kings, but we know Him as Friend. He is Lord of the Universe, yet we get to speak with Him in His private chambers.

Your testimony enables others to transfer their trust to Jesus Christ. The key to effective witnessing is not directing a message at someone, but rather, it is the transfer of the trust bond from one's own relationship with Christ to the other person.[1]

An individual is usually trusting in something for his eternal security. They have put their hopes in something temporal in order to give them a personal sense of identity and security. When we are appealing to them to yield in holy matrimony to Jesus Christ, they will be relinquishing their trust in religion, familiar ways, and earthly securities. Again, the question in the minds of many is, "Can your God be trusted?"

Noah built an altar after the flood. Similarly, Joshua took stones from each tribe to build a memorial unto the Lord after they had crossed the Jordan River and entered into the promised land. The altar and stone memorials were testimonies. These structures spoke to all of those who passed by of who God is, what He did, and what He will do. Today, we are the living stones (1 Pet. 2:5). We are built up in Christ as testimonials of who He is, what He has done, and what He will do.

As the Psalmist said, "Come and hear, all ye that fear God, and I will declare what He hath done for my soul" (Ps. 66:16). We can point out to the prospective bride many reasons why he can trust Jesus Christ. Obviously, He loved us to the point of death (John 3:16). We can share through Scripture the following facts; God is personal, God is a provider, and God answers prayers. However, **in order for the Word to be effective, it must be alive in us.** The Word must again take on flesh. Through his own experience, the servant demonstrated to Laban that the God whom he served was powerful, personal, and providential. He showed that God was alive and working right then in their midst and that He could be trusted.

In the letter to the saints at Thessalonica, Paul reminded them how he lived among them and how he imparted not only the gospel but also his own soul (1 Thess. 2:8). Paul preached with the demonstration of God's Spirit so that men would put their faith in God and not men (1 Cor. 2:5).

The servant approached Laban on the basis that God can be trusted. The personal testimony of God's working in both his and Abraham's life had an impact. The sense of urgency that the servant displayed about his mission was a testimony of faith. It said God is faithful, and He will do what He has promised. The generous giving of fine jewelry became a demonstration of God's power. It spoke to Laban that God is powerful, personal, and at work right now. Our lives should speak the same message to an unbelieving world. God is real. He is personal. He can be known and trusted. This is what people need in order to transfer their trust from the powers of darkness to the kingdom of light.

The most effective testimony is the one God is doing right now. It had to be obvious to Laban that God's hand had divinely maneuvered the events that brought the servant to his door. This is why it is so important to ask God to lead you in daily divine appointments.

The director of our discipleship house, Clint Matthews, went to minister one evening at the Brazos County Jail. He prayed and asked for God to lead him to those whom God had specifically prepared. Clint gave his testimony that night to a small group of prisoners.

Unknowingly, one prisoner, Levon Thomas, happened to be from the same small Texas town and matriculated at the same high school. Levon was a few years younger and knew Clint as a popular basketball star and party-goer. Hearing Clint's testimony of how God changed his life brought Levon to repentance. After his release, he joined the discipleship house, and he is now discipling others.

Meeting an old high school acquaintance years later in the county jail showed Levon that God had orchestrated the circumstance. The circumstance itself is a testimony to a living God who will personally send messengers to the unsaved.

Praying for divine appointments, I went witnessing door-to-door with a small group. The first door that I knocked on was that of a single parent whose son had participated in an activity with mine. I rarely talked to her before, but she let us in. I made it a point to let her know that God had arranged our meeting. We had chosen this neighborhood randomly. God had me choose her door as the first one to knock on.

The circumstances were arranged in such a way that we all knew God did it. Knowing the meeting was God ordained helped this woman to be open about the sin in her life and her need for the Savior. As you recognize that God is working daily in the events of your life with a living testimony, your faith increases, and you become more effective as a sower and a reaper of the end-time harvest.

The exciting part about these appointments is that you can retrace your steps, so you can let unbelievers know how God has divinely put the meetings together for the purpose of obtaining them as marriage partners for the Son of God. They can see that it is not a coincidence. They witness God's power and providence first hand. They are confronted with His reality and with His loving hand reaching out to them through you. By His grace, you will lead them in an exchange of vows where they commit themselves to their eternal partner, Jesus Christ.

17

Holy Boldness

And now if ye will deal kindly and truly
with my master, tell me: and if not,
tell me; that I may turn to the right hand,
or to the left.
—Genesis 24:49

After the servant's testimony which beautifully demonstrated the awesome hand of God that lead him to Rebekah, Eliezer boldly asks for what he has come for —the bride.

You may have many friends and relatives who have seen the divine intervention of God's hand in their lives. The purpose of God's involvement is to bring them into the kingdom, but they must realize this and obey.

Eliezer's faith was strengthened as he shared his testimony. It was obvious to him that God had chosen Rebekah and was reaching out to her family. At this point, the most unnatural thing would have been not to pointedly ask for a commitment. Unfortunately, that is what so many of us do.

We fail to present the gospel so that they can obey. After seeing God's hand in the lives of our loved ones, friends, or acquaintances through healing, prevention of an accident, or triumph in a circumstance that was beyond their ability, we fail to communicate that God's mercy has been reaching out to them so that they will become a part of His bride. Jesus invited people to follow Him, and we need to let people know of the invitation to be the bride of Christ and to fellowship with Him at the great wedding feast.

It is proper, in our culture, for a man to ask a woman for her hand in marriage. This is what we call "popping the question." Unless the man gains the courage to pop the question, he stands the chance of losing the love of his life.

We, the church, are acting on behalf of the bridegroom, Jesus Christ, and we are called to seek the hand of the prospective bride. We too must have the courage to "pop the question(s)." If we lack the courage, we run the risk of losing the love of Christ to the enemy.

After hearing of God's intervention, it was truly a question of obedience on Laban's part. It is a question of obedience to all who have received a revelation of God and have heard the Gospel:

> And to you who are troubled rest with us, when the Lord Jesus shall be revealed from heaven with his mighty angels, in flaming fire taking vengeance on them that know not God, and that obey not the gospel of our Lord Jesus Christ.　　　　(2 Thess. 1:7–8)

Paul's mission as stated in Romans 1:5 (NIV) is "to call people from among all the Gentiles to the obedience that comes from faith."

The question is our obedience. God commands all men to repent (Acts 17:30). He has invited mankind to accept His Son as Savior. He has commanded mankind to repent and to serve Jesus as Lord. We are God's ambassadors. We must let people know. It is a matter of obedience.

What are some of the things that possibly gave this servant the boldness to enter the home of a stranger and to call him to obey? First, *the servant had the right perspective* of what he had to offer to Rebekah. Perspective will give you boldness. It would be a privilege for anyone to be Isaac's bride and to have a father-in-law like Abraham. This is why the servant says in Genesis 24:49:

> And now if ye will deal kindly and truly with my master, tell me: and if not, tell me; that I may turn to the right hand, or to the left.

The servant knew that if Laban would not obey, the privilege would go to another. Isaac would have a bride.

Our perspective is much the same. We are bringing home a bride for the Lord, Jesus Christ. For those who will accept, they are becoming royalty, heirs of God, joint heirs in Christ, not to mention that they will miss eternity with the devil and his demons. It is a privilege to be Christ's bride. God will have his eternal companion. Those who will be blessed with this sacred union are those who are obedient by faith.

One night as I was witnessing outside a bar, three college students surrounded me and began to threaten me saying, "How would you like your face kicked in?"

I replied to them, "You certainly have the ability to do just that if you want. But before you do, let me share this one thing. If I was out here passing out football cards and bragging on the Dallas Cowboys, you would have your arms around me, buy me a beer, and be having a good old time. But, because I am passing out tracts about Jesus Christ, the Creator of the Universe, the Lord of heaven and earth, the Savior who died on the cross for your sins, you are ready to kick my face in. Do you see how wicked you are?" I was pointing my finger at them. They were stunned. Not knowing what to say but for a few curse words, they walked away.

This is not a recommended witnessing method, however, one of the reasons that I could boldly speak to them in the face of danger was because of the perspective that I had about what I was doing and whom I was serving. Paul asked for prayers from the church in Ephesus so that he would declare the gospel fearlessly as he should. This is how we should declare it: **boldly and without fear**. Paul was imprisoned as he wrote to the Ephesians. He was saying to the saints at Ephesus, "Do not let me compromise the message just because I am in prison and people may take my life."

The danger of compromise can be seen in the story about the hunter and the bear:

A hunter met a bear in the woods.
He lifted his rifle to shoot when the
bear said, "Wait, please do not shoot.

Perhaps we can talk. I know you want a fur coat, and all I want is lunch. Put down the gun, and let's see if we can't come to a compromise."

An hour later, the bear was sitting on a log belching from a full stomach. The hunter's gun was on the ground. The hunter was nowhere to be found. You see, they had come to a compromise. The hunter now had his fur coat, and the bear had his lunch.

Anytime we compromise the gospel, the devil is having us for lunch. In other words, he is getting the best of us and winning the battle for souls. For no reason, whether it be to save our own skin, to save our self-esteem in the face of rejection, or to fill the building, are we to lower the standard of the gospel. Paul said,

I am not ashamed of the gospel, for it is the power of God for salvation for everyone who believes; first to the Jew then the Gentile. (Romans 1:16)

Not only did the servant have perspective, but *he was in the perfect will of God*. Being in the perfect will of God will encourage us to share with God's confidence. The servant personally experienced Abraham's goodness and naturally shared how Rebekah, in becoming Isaac's bride, would enjoy the same fellowship. When the servant recalled how God providentially directed every step of his travel to the house of Laban, it confirmed to Eliezer that he was in God's perfect will. Knowing this, he challenged Laban to make his decision.

As you know, it is the Lord's will to sow the seed of the gospel. Winning souls is wise. It is the last word of our commanding officer, and as long as you are doing God's will, God's way, you will see God's hand which will give you courage to proclaim the gospel fearlessly. Being in God's will means that God's spirit specifically directs you to people he has prepared through others or through circumstances. You, knowing the events, sense God's direction and the presence of the Holy Spirit which enable you to share the gospel.

The servant was also well-prepared. Preparation will help us to be bold in our going. Preparation comes in the form of equipping. The servant was equipped with all the goods of Abraham. He was prepared with years of relationship with Abraham. It was natural for him to share about His master and the God whom he served. Remember, God has loaded us down with the gifts of the Spirit. They are at our disposal as we go. Our first preparation is to know Him in order to make Him known.

As we experience God, we become God-confident. As we receive instruction and use that instruction, the Lord will train us. The best way to learn to evangelize is by doing evangelism. I believe that the bride cannot make herself ready for the Lord's return apart from witnessing. For example, note some of the characteristics that are needed to be an effective witness. These same characteristics are what make you His bride. These are not developed in a Sunday school class or in a seminary. They are developed as we participate in our global occupation of bringing home the bride. We mature through our on-the-job training. The heart of the spiritual war is found in witnessing and not in the cool of a classroom. The very act of going out refines our character, making us ready for His return.

Being a witness requires that:

1. We know and love God. Evangelism deepens our love for God and our fellow man. If we do not know God, it is unlikely that we will sustain our witness very long.
2. We have the faith that overcomes fear.
3. We know God's Word and learn how to be led by the Spirit.
4. We will have to refine our character

so as not to discredit the message.

5. We learn how to pray His kingdom come. Prayer says that we humbly depend on God to give conviction, conversion, and life.

6. We are reminded to be continually grateful for His saving grace in our lives.

Our determined commitment to witness throws us to absolute dependence on God. To be what we ought to be in order to effectively share what we need to impart will take His presence and power working through us. In the whole process, God is sculpting us into His image, getting us ready to be His eternal partner.

The servant set apart Abraham as his master. Only as we set apart Christ as Lord will we be able to share Him boldly. Our sole motivation must be to see Jesus reign in every heart. If we are trying to promote our church, our ministry, or our denomination, the Spirit of God will not enable us. First Peter 3:15 states, "But sanctify the Lord God in your hearts." Why? So you may be able to give a reason for the hope that you have in Christ Jesus. Our hope is not in a denomination, doctrine, pastor, or local church but in Christ who died, arose, and lives forever.

Paul strove to keep a clear conscience before God and man (Acts 24:16). Paul had a pure motive for serving Jesus. He was not trying to prove to others that he was an apostle or a Christian. He shared because Jesus was the Lord of his life. Out of love for Jesus, he was compelled to share.

The Spirit enables those who exalt Jesus alone in their hearts to declare Jesus as Lord to the nations. If your motive is not pure, it may be why you have not been effective or have lacked the confidence and boldness to share with others. The righteous (those who are in right relationship) will be as bold as a lion.

Christ as Lord in your heart also means that you will be without fear of rejection. One who walks in the lordship of Jesus Christ knows that people are not rejecting him as a person, but they are rejecting the Lord. The perfect love of God will cast out such fears and free us up to share the gospel.

In order to witness, *we need to be filled with the Spirit*. Paul reminded Timothy, "For God hath not given us the spirit of fear; but of power, and of love, and of a sound mind" (2 Tim. 1:7).

The Holy Spirit is not shy. Paul quoting the Old Testament said, "I believe, therefore I speak." The natural result of being a believer is speaking of the Lord Jesus Christ. The Holy Spirit is given so that we will bear witness of Our Redeemer (Acts 1:8). The Apostles, after being imprisoned, had been given strict orders not to teach in the name of Jesus. They said that they could not help speaking about what they had seen and heard. If you are filled with the Spirit, Jesus must spill out of your heart and through your mouth. It is from the overflow of the heart that the mouth speaks. If Jesus is in by the Holy Spirit, Jesus must come out. This is not just for the super saints or the apostles but for all believers filled with the Holy Spirit. Acts 4:31 says,

> And when they had prayed, the place was shaken where they were assembled together; and they were all filled with the Holy Ghost, and they spake the Word of God with boldness.

When going out to witness, I often take my children with me. Leah, the oldest, has had the most exposure. The boldness to testify has rubbed off on her. She is very vocal about her faith.

One afternoon, we went shopping. Leah, only seven years old at the time, confronted an older gentleman at the check-out counter. She asked him, "Do you love Jesus?"

The older man, trying to placate my daughter, patted her on the head and said, "Yes, I love Jesus."

Sensing the lack of sincerity in his answer, Leah restated, "Do you really love Jesus?" The man could only grin, as he was embarrassed and hoped the gospel-bombadier's parents would quickly check out.

The Lord is not a respecter of persons. He has filled my young daughter with His words. He, too, will fill your heart to overflowing from your mouth. He has loaded down your camels, and boldness is on board. You can do all things through Christ who strengthens you. Open your mouth, and allow God to fill it. Each step of obedience in imparting Christ brings a greater experiential knowledge of Jesus Christ in our own lives and with it an increasing boldness to proclaim His Gospel. Equipped with this boldness, nothing will hinder us.

18

"Hinder Me Not"

*And he said unto them, Hinder me not, seeing
the LORD hath prospered my way; send me
away that I may go with my master.*
—Genesis 24:56

L aban wisely agreed to give Rebekah's
hand in marriage to Isaac. The servant
arose the next morning ready to return
to his master with the bride-to-be.

Laban and his mother were startled by
the servant's sense of urgency. They resisted
him saying, "Let the damsel abide with us a
few days, at the least ten; after that she shall
go" (Gen. 24:55).

What a temptation! After a long, arduous
trip, no one would expect this servant not to
have a break today. He deserved it.

In today's language, they were saying,
"What's your hurry? You've got Rebekah. Your
job is as good as done. Take it easy. Relax!"

The servant said unto them, "Hinder me not, seeing the LORD has prospered me."

The servant knew that his job was not completed until the bride was delivered to the bridegroom. Nothing was going to deter him from the task. Similarly for us, **evangelism is not finished until the bride sits down with the bridegroom at the wedding feast of the Lamb.** It would have been so easy for this servant to consider his own desires and needs. What hinders the work of evangelism in our world today is not Communism, humanism, or Islam, but it is selfishness.

In his book *True Discipleship*, William MacDonald points out that two out of three men who desired to follow Jesus in Luke 9:57–62 thought that they could take care of their personal business first. The excuses "Let me first…" and "Allow me to first…" reveal that they wanted "Me first." As MacDonald states, "'Lord, *me first'* is a moral absurdity and impossibility."[1]

Selfishness brings death to evangelism. Since evangelism is the life giving breath to the church, selfishness also kills the church. It will stifle and eventually kill the servants of evangelism as well.

One day, toward the close of World War II in a fashionable western home, the phone rang. The woman who answered heard the words, "Hi, Mom. I'm coming home." It was her sailor son just back from active duty. He was calling from San Diego. The mother was wild with joy. Her son was alive. He went on, "I'm bringing a buddy with me. He got hurt pretty bad. Only has one eye, one arm, and one leg. He has no home, and I'd sure like him to live with us."

The mother said, "Sure, son, he can stay with us for awhile."

"Mom, you do not understand. I want him to live with us always."

Said the mother, "Well, OK, we'll try it for a year."

"But, Mom, I want him to be with us always. He's in bad shape, one eye, one arm, one leg."

The mother got impatient. "You're too emotional about this. You've been in a war. The boy will be a drag on us."

The phone clicked and went dead. The next day, the parents received a telegram from the Navy. Their son had leaped to his death from the twelfth floor of a San Diego hotel. In a few days, the body was shipped home. When the casket was opened, the parents stared at their son's body. He had one eye, one arm, and one leg. With crushing pain came understanding. Fearing rejection, their son had phoned seeking acceptance. His mother's unwillingness to show love and to bear a burden had snapped his fragile will to live.

Selfishness is not simply unattractive. It is deadly.[2]

The other hindrance that has its root in selfishness is that of comfort. Jesus told us that we are to do one thing with self; crucify it! Without the cross, there is no Christianity. The Bible tells us to "throw off everything that would so easily entangle us." We, especially in America, are the most easily entangled group. We have an appetite for entertainment that the world has never seen. Sports, movies, TVs, video games, clubs, concerts, cruises—you name it, we have got it. The more that we indulge in these, the more we become prisoners to them until our appetite cannot be satisfied, and our hunger and zeal for God in evangelism is all but dead.

Raynald III was the grossly overweight Duke of Belgium. He was nicknamed "Raynald the fat." After a violent quarrel, Raynald's younger brother, Edward, led a successful revolt against him. Edward took his fat brother captive. He built a room around Raynald in the castle and promised him that he could regain his title and property as soon as he was able to leave the room.

This would not have been difficult for most people since the room had several windows and a door of near normal size, none of which were locked or barred. The problem was Raynald's size. To regain his freedom, he needed to lose weight. But, Edward knew his older brother, and each day, he sent a variety of delicious foods. Instead of dieting his way out of prison, Raynald grew fatter.

When Duke Edward was accused of cruelty, he had a ready answer, "My brother is not a prisoner. He may leave when he so wills." Raynald stayed in the room for ten years and eventually died a prisoner of his own appetite.

The church has been taken captive by worldly appetites, and the work of evangelism is also held prisoner. We must throw off the things that hinder (the gods of entertainment and comfort) and pursue Christ as never before.

Douglas Hyde was a card-carrying Communist before he turned to our Lord Jesus Christ. In his book *Dedication and Leadership*, he describes a typical day:

> Do you remember what life was really like in the Party? You got up in

the morning, and as you shaved, you were thinking of the jobs you would do for Communism that day. You went down to breakfast and read the *Daily Worker* to get the Party line—to get the shot and shell for a fight in which you were already involved. You read every item in the paper wondering how you might be able to use it for the cause.

I had never been interested in sport, but I read the sports pages in order to be able to discuss sport with others and to be able to say to them, "Have you read this in the *Daily Worker*?" I would follow this through by giving them the paper in the hope that they might turn from the sports pages and read the political ones too.

On the bus or train, on my way to work, I read the *Daily Worker* as ostentatiously as I could, holding it up so that others might read the headlines and perhaps be influenced by them. I took two copies of the paper with me; the second one I left on the seat in the hope that someone would pick it up and read it.

When I got to work, I kept the *Daily Worker* circulating. One worker after another would take it outside, read it for a few minutes, and bring it back to me again. At lunch time, in the canteen or the restaurant, I would try to start conversations with those with whom I was eating. I made a practice of sitting with different groups in order to spread my influence as widely as I could. I did not thrust Communism down their throats but steered our conversations in such a way that they could be brought round to politics or, if possible, to the campaigns which the Party was conducting at the time.

Before I left my place of work at night, there was a quick meeting of the factory group or cell. There we discussed in a few minutes the successes and failures of the day. And we discussed, too, what we hoped to be able to do on the following day.

I dashed home, had a quick meal, and then went out, maybe to attend classes, maybe to be a tutor, maybe to join some Communist campaign, going from door to door canvassing or standing at the side of the road selling Communist papers—doing something for Communism. And I went home at night and dreamed of the jobs I was going to do for Communism the next day.[3]

Here is a man who was totally committed to successfully persuading people to a dead

Communism. What could we achieve in Christ if our main passion was to win people to an alive Savior and not to see how comfortable we can get? Many aspects of our life are motivated by comfort. The more things that we acquire to make us comfortable, the more we are enslaved by them. From the repairing of our boats to the manicuring of our lawns, it captures our time and money to the sacrifice of Christ's work on earth.

One other major hindrance is that of our family ties. God allows the people closest to us to test our love for Him. Our earthly affections can never supersede our love for the master and His work. There is nothing wrong with taking care of the family. The family is designed to be a helpmate for the work of the gospel, and it should be nurtured. It is when those family members seek to hinder God's purposes by holding onto their selfish desires that we are obligated to move ahead in Christ.

Laban and his mother sought to do just that. There was no need for the servant to stay. The Lord's providence was obvious, but it was the emotional loss of her daughter that the mother did not want to face, and she was intent on delaying it as long as she could.

It was for this reason that Jesus said in Luke 14:33, "So likewise, whosoever he be of you that forsaketh not all that he hath, he cannot be my disciple." Our love for Jesus Christ must be supreme in comparison to others. He is Lord of all or not at all.

When I told my family that I was committing my life to Christ and was being baptized, they were upset and asked me not to leave the religion in which I was raised. I told them, "Do not look at it as if I'm leaving your religion. See me as going on with Christ." Following Jesus always means leaving something or someone behind.

When I made the decision to go into ministry, I faced opposition from family members again. "Being a Christian is one thing," they would argue, "but going off to Bible college to be a priest or whatever means that you have totally flipped." I am happy to report that God has changed my family and their outlook.

Again in going to Nigeria, West Africa, the people who opposed us were those who were a part of the family of God. We returned to the U.S. with hardships and sickness. Our commitment to return again was resisted. "You have such a beautiful family. How can you take five sweet kids there? What if they die?" I could lose my children, but they will never be lost. As Jim Elliot, a martyred missionary to Ecuador, said, "He is no fool who gives up what he cannot keep to gain what he cannot lose."

This life and its comfort is not the goal. "For to me to live is Christ, and to die is gain" (Phil. 1:21). I am shocked by elders and deacons who object the longest and loudest when their children desire to get into foreign missions or inner-city work. Many have raised their children with the selfish motivation of knowing the good life. They should raise them with the motivation of releasing them to Christ, so after our parental teaching, He may use them however He sees fit.

Maintain an unhindered life. Throw off the easy entanglements of comfort and entertainment. Say no to worldly affections that seek to supersede Christ's love and call on your life. Rebuke the voice that says, "preserve this life at all cost." "Hinder me not," says the servant whose goal is not this life. His goal is pleasing his Master by bringing home a bride for the Lord, Jesus Christ.

Remember, evangelism is not finished until the bride sits down with the bridegroom at the wedding feast of the Lamb.

The unhindered servant will walk triumphantly in God's victory parade with multitudes. Until then, **"Hinder me not."**

19

Thousands of Millions

And they blessed Rebekah, and said unto her,
Thou art our sister, be thou the mother of
thousands of millions, and let thy seed possess
the gate of those which hate them.
And Rebekah arose, and her damsels, and
they rode upon the camels, and followed the
man: and the servant took Rebekah,
and went his way.
—Genesis 24:60–61

They eventually conceded to let Rebekah go but not without their blessing. "And they blessed Rebekah, and said unto her, 'Thou art our sister, be thou the mother of thousands of millions, and let thy seed possess the gate of those which hate them'" (Gen. 24:60).

Rebekah's blessing is a prophetic utterance confirming God's promises to Abraham. Genesis 12:3 states, "In thee shall all families of the earth be blessed." The following passages show more of God's promises and blessings to Abraham:

> And I will make thy seed as the dust of the earth: so that if a man can number the dust of the earth, then shall thy seed also be numbered.   (Gen. 13:16)

> That in blessing I will bless thee, and in multiplying I will multiply thy seed as the stars of the heaven, and as the sand which is upon the sea shore; and thy seed shall possess the gate of his enemies.   (Gen. 22:17)

The promise of Abraham is being fulfilled today. Jesus will have His church. David Barret documented that from 1968 to 1988 over 268 million people came to know Jesus Christ as Lord and Savior. The majority of those salvations took place outside of western Europe and the U.S.[1]

We do not have to wait for the harvest; the harvest is here. Bring out the sickle of God's Word, swing it by the power of the Holy Spirit, and reap. The Lord is building the new Jerusalem. In His Father's house are many mansions. God's *many* equals thousands of millions. Abraham's seed could not be numbered. Revelation 7:9 describes that seed: "After this I beheld, and, lo, a great multitude." I love this. The apostle John gets a revelation of the great heavenly throng of believers around the throne. He is overwhelmed, "I beheld, and, lo." That's our version of "Awesome! Unbelievable! Look at all the people!" It is:

> A great multitude, which no man could number, of all nations, and kindreds, and people, and tongues, stood before the throne, and before the Lamb.
>
> (Rev. 7:9)

Four thousand years later, John writes what was foretold to Abraham and Rebekah. We are living in this reality today as we reap the end-time harvest of souls. What motivates us in a dark world is the hope we have in the victory made certain by our Lord Jesus Christ. What gave the servant confidence was that he was on a mission that God Himself promised was going to succeed. Before leaving, Eliezer asks Abraham what to do if the woman is not willing to follow him. Abraham responds,

> The LORD God of heaven, which took me from my father's house, and from the land of my kindred, and which

spake unto me, and that swear unto me, saying, Unto thy seed will I give this land; he shall send his angel before thee, and thou shalt take a wife unto my son from thence. (Gen. 24:7)

The angel guaranteed that he should take a wife, and Jesus guaranteed that He will build His church. The second half of the blessing corresponds with what Jesus said about his triumphant church. The blessing in Genesis 24:60 adds, "and let thy seed possess the gate of those which hate them." Matthew 16:18 similarly states, "I will build my church; and the gates of hell shall not prevail against it." The church will be prevailing against the gates of hell. As Reinhard Bohnke's book title says, we are *Plundering Hell to Populate Heaven*. These Scriptures are being fulfilled, as the plundering is taking place, like never before. We are speedily coming to the close of the earth's history as the harvest is being reaped.

According to Francis Frangipane,

Today, Christianity is growing three times faster than the world's population. Every day, more than 178,000 people come into the kingdom of God. Twenty-eight thousand new converts daily confess Jesus as Lord in communist China. According to *Reader's Digest*, entire cities are being won to Christ: twenty thousand people a day in Africa, thirty-five thousand souls a day in Latin America.

More than seventy percent of the progress in world evangelization from the time of Christ until today has occurred since 1900. Seventy percent of that has occurred since World War II, and seventy percent of that has occurred in the last three years. In India, there are more than eighty-five million believers. More people have turned to the Lord in Muslim Iran in the last ten years than the previous thousand.

Almost entire populations of Kurdish cities have been converted as a result of the Gulf War. In 1991, during the annual pilgrimage to Mecca, a number of Muslim Mullahs from Nigeria were praying inside the grand Mosque when Jesus appeared to them and declared that He was the Son of God. They all were converted to Christianity.

U.S.A. Today reported that there are more Christians in Russia than in the United States. Officials say that fifty-five percent of all Russian teachers are professing to be Christians.[2]

The multitudes who are coming to Christ are not only a fulfillment of the prophecy made by Rebecca's mother, but they are also the fulfillment of Zechariah 8:23. This passage describes the end-time revival and subsequent harvest:

> Thus saith the Lord of hosts; In those days it shall come to pass, that ten men shall take hold out of all languages of the nations, even shall take hold of the skirt of Him that is a Jew, saying, We will go with you: for we have heard that God is with you.   (Zech. 8:23)

The ten men in verse 23 again represent a fullness or completeness. It speaks of all languages and nations worldwide grasping the sleeve of the robe of a Jew saying, "We will go with you: for we have heard that God is with you." Who is that Jew? It is Jesus. The Jesus in you and me; we have been clothed in His righteousness. People will see Jesus in us and will take a hold of us because they see God is with (and in) us. The ultimate worldwide **attract attack** is coming and is here! Multitudes are taking hold of the sleeve of the Jew, Jesus. The fullness of the Gentiles is coming in. Every knee shall bow; the Lord is building His church.

Thus saith the Lord of hosts; If it be marvellous in the eyes of the remnant of this people in these days, should it also be marvellous in mine eyes? saith the Lord of hosts.   (Zech. 8:6)

If we see the great harvest's coming as marvelous, how much more marvelous for the Lord Jesus who has waited two thousand years to sit down with His bride at the wedding feast of the Lamb. The ending of the Song of Songs prophesies of this conclusion of the marriage between the bridegroom and the bride. And this is our blissful end:

[Joyfully the radiant bride turned to him, the one altogether lovely, the chief among ten thousand to her soul, and with unconcealed eagerness to begin her life of sweet companionship with him, she answered] Make haste, my beloved, and come quickly, like a gazelle or a young hart [and take me to our waiting home] upon the mountains of spices!   (Song of Sol. 8:14, AMP)

So, Jesus Christ will have His bride. Will you be a part of this last gathering of souls before our Lord returns? Will you know the reward and privilege of bringing home a bride for our Lord and Savior. Victory is certain. His promises are sure, and He's loaded down our camels.

If you love Him, you will obey the Father and the Son's command to "Go," so that the Spirit and the bride may soon say, "Come, Lord Jesus."

END NOTES

CHAPTER 1
1. George E. Sweazy, "Hiding from God behind Religion," *Presbyterian Life* (September 1968).
2. Paul Billheimer, *Destined for the Throne* (Minneapolis: Bethany House, 1975), 25–26.

CHAPTER 2
1. William MacDonald, *True Discipleship* (Benin City: Maranatha, 1963), 65.
2. Charles G. Trumball, *Taking Men Alive* (London: Letterworth Press, 1957), 7.

CHAPTER 3
1. Keith Green, "Zeal: The Good, The Bad, and The Ugly," *Last Days Magazine* 16 (March 1993): 22.
2. David S. Kirkwood, *Your Best Year Yet* (Lake Mary: Creation House, 1990), 27.

CHAPTER 4
1. John White, *The Parable of the Orange Tree*, from the author's personal collection.

CHAPTER 5
1. C.F. Keil and F. Delitzsch, *Keil-Delitzcsh Commentary on the Old Testament* Vol. 1. (Grand Rapids: Wm. B. Eerdmans Publishing, 1980), 257.
2. Ruth Tucker, *From Jerusalem to Iran Jaya* (Grand Rapids: Zondervan, 1983), 27.

CHAPTER 6

1. Ed Silvoso, *That None Should Perish* (Ventura: Regal Books, 1994), 96.
2. Robert H. Stein, *The Method and Message of Jesus' Teaching* (Philadelphia: Westminster Press, 1978), 82.
3. *Open Bible: New American Standard Version* (Nashville: Thomas Nelson, 1983), 1298.
4. William MacDonald, *True Discipleship* (Benin City: Maranatha, 1963), 26–27.
5. Leighton Ford, *Good News Is for Sharing* (Elgin: David C. Cook Publishing, 1977), 106.

CHAPTER 7

1. Sheldon Vanauken, *A Severe Mercy* (New York: Harper and Row, 1977), 85.
2. Joe Maxwell, "A Conspiracy of Kindness," *Charisma* 19, no. 5 (December 1993).
3. Ruth Tucker, *From Jerusalem to Iran Jaya* (Grand Rapids: Zondervan, 1983), 21.

CHAPTER 8

1. John Wimber, *Power Evangelism* (San Francisco: Harper and Row, 1986), 57.
2. C. Peter Wagner, *Your Spiritual Gifts Can Help Your Church Grow* (Ventura: Regal, 1979), 111–135.

CHAPTER 9

1. Rick Joyner, *The Harvest* (Springdale: Whitaker House, 1993), 82.
2. Ibid., 84–85.
3. George Caywood, *Escaping Materialism* (Sisters, Oregon: Questar, 1989), 60.
4. John Calvin, *Sermons on II Samuel*, Trans. by Douglas Kelly (Carlisle: Banner of Truth Trust, 1992), 202.
5. Ruth Tucker, *From Jerusalem to Iran Jaya* (Grand Rapids: Zondervan, 1983), 26.

6. David Barrett and Todd Johnson, *Our Globe and How to Reach It* (Birmingham: New Hope, 1990), 27.

7. Doug Lucas, "A Vision for World Missions—Valley View Style," *Christian Standard* 128 (May 30, 1993).

8. George Otis, Jr., *The Last of the Giants* (Tarrytown: Chosen Books, 1991), 240.

9. David Barrett and Todd Johnson, 25.

CHAPTER 10

1. Ray Comfort, *Hell's Best Kept Secret* (Springdale: Whitaker, 1989), 25.

2. Ibid., 23.

3. Dr. James Kennedy, *Evangelism Explosion Revised Edition* (Wheaton, Illinois.: Tyndale House Publishing, 1977), 26–27.

4. Ray Comfort, *Words of Comfort: Syllabus* on *Radical Evangelism* (Privately published), 6.

CHAPTER 11

1. Ed Silvoso, *That None Should Perish* (Ventura: Regal Books, 1994), 247.

2. John Robb, "Prayer as a Strategic Weapon in Frontier Missions," *Society for Frontier Missiology* (September 13–15, 1990).

3. Exerpted from a sermon by Leonard Ravenhill.

4. George Otis, Jr., *The Last of the Giants* (Tarrytown: Chosen Books, 1991), 248.

CHAPTER 12

1. "Testimony of Andrew Merry," provided by Doug Stringer (Turning Point Ministries, Houston, Texas).

2. John Wimber, *Power Evangelism* (San Francisco: Harper and Row, 1986), 51.

3. Terry Wardle, *One to One* (Camphill: Christian Publications, 1989), 104.

CHAPTER 13
1. Dr. and Mrs. Howard Taylor, *J. Hudson Taylor, God's Man in China: A Biography* (Chicago: Moody Press, 1987), 49.
2. Ibid., 50.
3. Dick Eastman, *Change the World School of Prayer: Basic Manual* (Colorado Springs: Every Home for Christ, 1983) 85.
4. Ibid., 85.
5. Norman Lewis, *Priority One: What God Wants* (Orange: Promise, 1988), 73.
6. Ibid., 100.

CHAPTER 16
1. Marvin K. Mayers, *Christianity Confronts Culture: A Study for Cross Cultural Evangelism* (Grand Rapids: Zondervan, 1987), 23.

CHAPTER 18
1. William MacDonald, *True Discipleship* (Benin City: Maranatha, 1963), 26.
2. Norman Lewis, *Priority One: What God Wants* (Orange: Promise Books, 1988), 110.
3. Douglas Hyde, *Dedication and Leadership* (Notre Dame: University of Notre Dame Press, 1966), 22–23.

CHAPTER 19
1. Dow Robinson, *Introduction to Missions Class,* Liberty Theological Seminary, Videotape, vol. 1.
2. Francis Frangipane, *1994 Pastors' Conference: Francis Frangipane Address,* Audiotape recorded at Aldergate United Methodist Church, College Station, Texas (April 24, 1994).

ACKNOWLEDGMENTS

My sincerest thanks to these publishers and ministries for their generous permission to use the following:

DEDICATION AND LEADERSHIP by Douglas Hyde
Copyright © 1966
University of Notre Dame Press, Notre Dame, Ind. 46556

"HIDING FROM GOD BEHIND RELIGION" by George E. Sweazy
September 1968
Presbyterian Life magazine, Louisville, Ky. 40202
Used with permission from the Presbyterian Church (USA).

YOUR SPIRITUAL GIFTS CAN HELP YOUR CHURCH GROW by C. Peter Wagner
Copyright © 1979
Regal Books, Ventura, Calif. 93003

POWER EVANGELISM by John Wimber and Kevin Springer
Copyright © 1986
Harper Collins Publishers, New York, N.Y. 10022

J. HUDSON TAYLOR, GOD'S MAN IN CHINA: A BIOGRAPHY by Dr. and Mrs. Howard Taylor
Copyright © 1987
Moody Bible Institute of Chicago Moody Press, Chicago, Ill.

PRIORITY ONE: WHAT GOD WANTS by Norman Lewis
Copyright © 1988
Promise Publishing, Miami, Fla.
Used with permission of author.

HELL'S BEST KEPT SECRET by Ray Comfort
Copyright © 1989
Whitaker House, Springdale, Pa. 15144

OUR GLOBE AND HOW TO REACH IT by David B. Barrett
and Todd Johnson
Copyright © 1990
New Hope, Birmingham, Ala.

Used with permission of Global Desk—FMB

THE LAST OF THE GIANTS by George Otis, Jr.
Copyright © 1991
Chosen Books, Lynnwood, Wash. 98036

A VISION FOR WORLD MISSIONS by Doug Lucas
Copyright © 1993
Team Expansion
The Standard Publishing Company, Cincinnati, Ohio 45231

"A CONSPIRACY OF KINDNESS"
December 1993
Charisma magazine, Lake Mary, Fla. 32746

THAT NONE SHOULD PERISH by Ed Silvoso
Copyright © 1994
Regal Books, Ventura, Calif. 93003

*1994 PASTORS' CONFERENCE: FRANCIS FRANGIPANE
ADDRESS* by Francis Frangipane
Audiotape recorded April 24, 1994, at
Aldersgate United Methodist Church, College Station, Tex.
Used by permission of Renewal Ministries, Inc.

*CHANGE THE WORLD SCHOOL OF PRAYER BASIC
MANUAL* by Dick Eastman
Copyright © 1995
Mission Hills, Calif.
Reprint of 1983 manual
Currently published by Every Home for Christ
Colorado Springs, Colo. 80935-3595

LEONARD RAVENHILL SERMON
Exerpt used by permission of Bethany House Publishers, Minneapolis, Minn. 55438